This edition reproduces th
corrections, hosted at ht
future/.

MW00619074

Spengler's Future

An Outline of the Next Seven Centuries of Western History, as Suggested by Comparison with the Life Cycles of Four Other Civilizations

Paperback version published 2023 by With Both Hands Publishing, LLC.

Permission to republish the works of John J. Reilly by With Both Hands Publishing, LLC has been granted by the estate of John J. Reilly.

ISBN: 978-1-961310-00-1

With Both Hands Publishing
446 E Twelve Oaks Drive
Flagstaff, AZ 86005

https://www.benespen.com/

ben@benespen.com

**With Both
Hands
Publishing**

Table of Contents

Foreword

This is a report on the output of a computer program. The program was written to predict the future of the world, from a Western perspective, into the twenty-seventh century A.D. The program does not purport to predict specific events that will occur in time to come. Rather, it seeks to suggest events from many times and places in the past which could be analogous to what will be happening at designated points in the future. This is accomplished by using a simple cyclical model of the development of civilizations. The title of the report alludes to the fact that the model in question is an adaptation of the theory of history created by the German philosopher, Oswald Spengler, particularly as expressed in his great work, The Decline of the West.

Readers should note that Spengler never tried to "predict" the future in anything like the detail attempted here. The "future" outlined in this study can be said to really be Spengler's, in fact, only to the extent that some of it was implicit in his ideas. He can hardly be held responsible for most of what you will read here, since his philosophy was "adapted" for the program by being reduced to four lines of algorithms.

Although the program contains hundreds of data lines from various points in the histories of four civilizations, the output is no more self-explanatory than the hexagrams of the I Ching or a laying of tarot cards. To note that a battle occurred on such and such a date in a given civilization tells you almost nothing; you must know what part it played in the history of the culture in question for it to make any sense. Therefore, most of the text, like a good fortuneteller's patter, consists of the author's own interpretation of what the Delphic echoes from the past produced by the computer might someday represent. The method throughout, with the one exception described immediately below, is to look for harmonies and dissonances among the events from the past described in the output lines. The output lines themselves are given for each segment of the future to which they refer. The length of each segment was suggested to the author by apparent "themes" in consecutive groups of lines. (The temptation to edit them to make them fit better into their segments has been largely resisted.) Readers may therefore construct their own futures by seeing what these lines suggest to them.

An amusing feature of the output is that it attempts to "predict" the nineteenth and twentieth centuries (along with a cursory look at the last half of the eighteenth). The accompanying commentary attempts, with perhaps limited success, to treat these output lines in almost the same fashion as the lines dealing with the distant future are treated. However, it was not quite possible to avoid alluding to events in actual Western history which occurred during these centuries. Since the pattern has been established of using Western events as points of comparison, the commentary for future segments continues the procedure by mentioning imaginary future events of the author's devising. These are deliberately conservative suggestions, inserted for stylistic reasons. They should not be taken seriously.

As a matter of fact, these invented events do not closely resemble the future which the author himself anticipates. That future has far more in common with the ideas of Teilhard de Chardin (or at least Teilhard in his more Augustinian moments) than with those of Oswald Spengler. This book, indeed, can be taken as an attempt to exorcise a private nightmare. At least in the author's mind, this is what will happen if Teilhard and similar optimists turn out to be wrong. Despite its fantastic elements, you will be looking at a "realist" version of the future, the one we will get if the future is like the past.

In the Introduction which follows, Spengler's system is discussed in more detail than the program uses. We also consider the more general question of whether a cyclical view of history can be seriously defended. Readers who are not much interested in this kind of question may confine themselves to reading just the highlighted passages in the Introduction, which simply reproduce the somewhat whimsical Instruction section of the program. Following the Introduction are the Antechronicles themselves (that is, chronicles written before the events they describe). As you will see, these are no more than fiction cobbled together from some historical analogies. They can be "right" only to the extent of being apt metaphors.

Finally, it should be understood that the program in question is a very crude piece of work (written in BASIC!) which really only saved the author a bit of simple arithmetic. It has no nifty graphics and will not be in the stores any time soon.

--John J. Reilly
August 1992

Introduction to Dr. Spengler's Temporal Analogizer

If you load the program, the old machine will peep and mutter after the fashion of its kind. Then, after some copyright notices relating to the underlying software appear on the screen, the program begins with the cheerful greeting:

Welcome to Dr. Spengler's Temporal Analogizer.

A somewhat fishy beginning, perhaps. Certainly it does not evoke great expectations of meticulous and dispassionate scholarship. It suggests, rather, carnival barkers and patent medicines, fortunetellers with the cunning of successful psychotherapists, and paperback reprints of the prophecies of Nostradamus with garishly colored covers depicting a fierce-eyed bearded lunatic. Indeed, the very self-deprecation raises even deeper concerns. It is obviously an attempt to get you to lower your guard. Very likely, the program is designed to induce a false sense of security in its users.

Before it is possible to make a firm assessment, however, another message rises onto the screen as the first disappears:

If you would like an explanation of the theory behind the program, please type '1' and press 'return.' If not, type '2' and press 'return.'

Though life is too short to read all the instructions offered to you, particularly the ones offered by computer programs, this

1

situation obviously requires some explanation. Therefore, you pick the first option, and the computer soon explains:

Dr. Spengler's Temporal Analogizer can predict the future into the 27th century.

The range for the program is not arbitrary. The early 27th century is about where the analogies from past civilizations which might some day apply to the West run out. Of course, how it can be said that analogies from, say, ancient Egypt run out at a distant point in the future is a matter which will require more explanation still. Before providing it, however, the program moves on to address some preliminary questions:

Dr. Spengler's Temporal Analogizer is based on the ideas of the German philosopher, Oswald Spengler (1880-1936).

Oswald Spengler was a secondary school mathematics teacher who achieved world fame on the strength of one of history's most improbable best-selling books. Spengler's doctorate was in Classical Greek philosophy, with a doctoral dissertation on the philosopher Heraclitus. (It should also be noted that Spengler's understanding of mathematical theory was formidable; his ability to treat mathematics as a characteristic product of a given culture and time may have been unique.) His own philosophy, strongly influenced by Nietzsche, bore more than a passing resemblance to the ideas of Martin Heidegger (who, like Spengler, would also become a supporter of the Nazis).

In the original version of the book, I said simply that Spengler had become a Nazi. I had in fact believed that Spengler was a nominal member of the National Socialist Party, until I was challenged by a reader on this point. A review of my sources (notably Spengler's Letters and Alasdair Hamilton's The Appeal

*of Fascism) reveals no evidence of membership, though there is
no doubt that Spengler was a sometime supporter of the party for
tactical reasons.*

A few years before the First World War, Spengler came into
an inheritance which permitted him to quit teaching school and
to pursue a historical study which he long had in mind, an
examination of the parallels between the Western Europe of the
early twentieth century and the Classical Mediterranean world at
the time of the Punic Wars between Rome and Carthage
(roughly, from the mid-third century B.C. to the mid-second
century B.C.). The outbreak of the First World War confirmed
him in his opinion that Western civilization had entered a period
of great wars of annihilation. It also came to deprive him of most
of his income, since the inheritance which had subsidized his
studies was largely in the form of income from stock in
American companies which were eventually forbidden to pay
dividends to Germans.

Nothing daunted and with Hannibal at the gates, Spengler
had the first volume of his masterpiece, Der Untergang des
Abendlandes, ready for publication just as Germany effectively
surrendered to the allies in 1918. (The second volume appeared
during the disastrous early 1920s.) Called The Decline of the
West in English, this book became extraordinarily sought after
throughout the German-speaking world, and then controversial
throughout the whole world in various translations. Even during
the great Weimar inflation, when each issue of money would
become worthless after a few days, Spengler became wealthy
just on sales in Switzerland alone. He wrote several more brief
books (such as Man and Technics and Prussianism and
Socialism) which simply expanded on points raised in his
magnum opus.

Why any book becomes popular is fundamentally mysterious, particularly when the book is long and deals in large part with remote or abstract matters. However, the attraction of Spengler's ideas seems to have been firmly based on the fact that he made it possible even for bad historical experience to make sense, something that the endlessly ameliorative models of history from the nineteenth century could not do. It is not true, as is often implied when The Decline of the West is mentioned, that Spengler thought the West was collapsing or would soon be overcome by outsiders. Far from it, as you shall see.

Spengler was a German nationalist, or perhaps just a naive patriot. At any rate, he looked forward to a war which would erase the humiliation of 1918, and he believed that democracy did not have much of a future. He was willing to support the Nazis until a pragmatic regime came along which would support the mix of state socialism and cultural traditionalism which he thought was the shape of things to come. He does not appear to have been either a racist in general or an antisemite in particular. For what it is worth, it can be noted that after the Nazis came to power he repeatedly made disparaging remarks about Hitler in public and by preference kept company with nationalist-conservatives, many of whom did not survive the regime. It is quite likely that his unexpected death from a heart attack in 1936 saved him from eventual arrest or execution.

The program pedantically proceeds from biography to ideology:

Dr. Spengler believed that civilizations go through life cycles of about the same duration, and that each civilization goes through similar phases.

Spengler divided up the life phases of civilizations in different ways, depending on whether he was talking about their

4

artistic life, political history, or spiritual life (the latter covering, roughly, philosophy and religion). To put all the possible periods together, he makes mention of:

A precultural period, when people are essentially barbarians, as was the case in what is usually called the Dark Ages of Europe;

Spring, an age of faith like the High Middle Ages in Europe;

Summer, like the Renaissance and early Baroque, when the culture develops its distinctive arts and sciences;

Autumn, when the fundamental insights of the culture reach full maturity (if not necessarily final form), as in late seventeenth and eighteenth century Europe; and

Winter, when the creations of the past in art and science and spiritual life are perfected and elaborated, but not fundamentally extended. Technology flourishes here, rather than fundamentally new science. For Spengler the science of the nineteenth and early twentieth centuries was not essentially new, because it was in the characteristically Western style of science established by people like Newton and Leibnitz. This final age is the time of increase in quantity, not quality. Spengler called Spring, Summer and Autumn "Culture," while Winter was the era of "Civilization" in his special sense of the term. The computer program, and so this book, are concerned exclusively with Winter.

Keep in mind that this outline distorts Spengler's ideas because it mentions only Western examples. His method was to find examples of the art or political life of the "Spring," for instance, from a variety of peoples and cultures. Thus, the pyramids of the Old Kingdom period in Egypt and the cathedrals of the High Middle Ages in Europe are both characteristic products of the Spring. He treated these illustrations as all of equal significance in their own stories, not as part of a great story leading up to the modern West.

Perhaps the most disconcerting premise of Spengler's for many readers will be his assertion that "modern times," roughly the early Winter of Western civilization beginning at the end of the eighteenth century, is not unique. Other civilizations have also experienced comparable periods of secularism and aggressively individual art and revolutionary politics, though each in its own form. Perhaps Spengler owed a lot of his popularity to the prediction that this kind of thing does not go on forever.

Neither, thankfully, does the program, which can now become more specific about how it operates:

When a person occupies the same place in the life cycle of one civilization as someone else does in another civilization's cycle, these people are said to be 'contemporary.' For instance, Spengler (and other historians) say that Alexander the Great in Classical times and Napoleon in the modern West are 'contemporary.'

There are several "other historians" who might be mentioned in this context, since Spengler has not had this kind of history all to himself, even in the twentieth century. His chief competitor as a comparative historian was the English scholar, Arnold Toynbee. The latter's great work, A Study of History, began to appear in 1934 and ultimately reached twelve volumes by the time it was completed in 1961. Toynbee, like Spengler, was convinced that the modern West was repeating, in its own style, much of the behavior of the ancient Greek and Roman civilization. Toynbee, however, did not see the cycles as in quite the same relationship as Spengler did. Toynbee believed that the First World War in the West was "contemporary" with the

Peloponnesian War between Athens and Sparta in ancient Greece, which occurred more than 200 years before the Punic Wars which so impressed Spengler. More generally, Toynbee did not believe in the fairly rigid cycles of Spengler's imagination. Toynbee's Study was explicitly intended as a British empiricist's correction of the German's dogmatic Decline. Among other things Spengler never attempted, the Study made a serious, indeed earnest, effort to cover the whole world. Toynbee would note the parallels and common patterns in the lives of different civilizations when they could be documented, but he refused to believe that history had ever been predestined, or that the fate of the West was already sealed. Events could always be traced to some individual or collective act of will.

The result was that Toynbee's history was built around certain loose sociological generalizations, notably his notion that historical change was a matter of "challenge" and "response." Since counter-examples to Toynbee's illustrations of these principles were always available, historians since the late 1950s (when Toynbee was the most famous of their number in the world, thanks to the patronage of Henry Luce at Time magazine) have been able to dismiss Toynbee because his explanations did not quite hold up, even if no one ever succeeded in explaining away the empirical historical parallels he described.

Toynbee's efforts can be considered a real advance on Spengler's, since Toynbee recognized that the different civilization cycles were obviously related to each other and fell into certain classes. Both historians recognize Greco-Roman (or "Classical") civilization as distinct from the more properly so-called "Western civilization" which arose in Western and Central Europe during the Dark Ages after the fall of the Roman Empire. Spengler said that the two societies had nothing in common but a partial coincidence of territory and some inessential technology.

Toynbee, on the other hand, insisted that Western Culture was obviously a successor to ("apparented by") the Classical world. He also pointed out that, while the Classical world was the creature of a certain limited geographical region, the West was at least in principle a "universal" civilization, a characteristic it shared with China (which also had a "classical" forerunner followed by a Dark Age) and with Islam. In comparison to both these latter generations of civilization, the earliest civilizations, which in Eurasia arose in river valleys, were really very local developments. Egypt, to take an example employed by the program, was never more than a small country. Still, even these early societies seemed to manifest many of the crises and phases which their later regional and universal descendants also experienced.

Finally, it must be noted that one of Toynbee's chief preoccupations was what he called "universal states." This is the final political form into which civilizations tend to fall. While Spengler was also keenly conscious of this final stage of his Winter phase of the historical cycle, he did not discuss the universal states in great detail. The program, on the other hand, deals primarily with the universal state phase of the West's cycle. After all, the program was designed to foretell the future, and almost the only part of the West's cycle still left to be played out is its destiny as a universal state.

Another slight delay, and the screen further explains:

Dr. Spengler's Temporal Analogizer selects events from the histories of past civilizations which will be "contemporary" to events in our future.

Which civilizations are we talking about? The ones from which data lines have been entered are ancient Egypt (from the Hyskos to the XXII Dynasty), China (from the Hegemony of

Chin to the end of the Latter Han Dynasty), the Classical world (from Alexander to the end of the Roman Empire), and a peculiar hybrid creature called "Islam." Spengler held that by the beginning of the Christian Era, the Middle East was the home of an awakening new culture which he called "Magian," after the Magi of ancient Persia. Spengler's idea was that the culture was composed of religious communities the way that the later West would be composed of "nation states" (an idea suggested, perhaps, by the ethnically-based administrative practices of the Ottoman Empire). Thus, the Jews, the Christians of Syria and Anatolia, and the Zoroastrians of Persia were all "Magian" communities. The birth of this new culture was masked, however, by the accident that the Romans had political control over much of its territory.

The distortion was as great as if the Arabs had conquered Merovingian France, imposing Arabic culture and art on people who had not yet had time to create their own. (Spengler calls this kind of distortion "pseudomorphosis," and says that much the same thing happened to Russia.) The new society had to express itself in alien forms; it pretended to be Greek and Roman. The Byzantine Empire, the successor to the Roman Empire of the East, was in reality a Magian polity. It was not essentially different in spirit from its long-time foe, Sassanid Persia, or more importantly, from the Islamic "Reformation" which ultimately destroyed it. This culture reached its final form in the Ottoman Empire, which collapsed as recently as the end of the First World War.

You do not have to accept Spengler's hypothesis of a "Magian culture" to see why the Ottoman Empire was included as one of the four sample civilizations: like Han China, the Roman Empire, and the Empire phase of Egyptian history, it lasted roughly 500 years and went through many of the same crises which these other empires also experienced. It was arguably a "universal state," since it swallowed a whole international system when it conquered the Middle East. The question is whether it can really be said to represent the final form of a single, mature "culture."

The program, however, can proceed undaunted by this kind of reservation to assure you:

It's as simple as that.

Indeed, it's even simpler than that. The complete edition of The Decline of the West (in English) appears in two thick volumes which together come to upwards of 800 pages, plus charts and indices. Dr. Spengler's Temporal Analogizer, on the other hand, is essentially embodied in four program lines, which read:

If E\$ = "China" then let H = F + 2300
If E\$ = "Egypt" then let H = F + 3547
If E\$ = "Rome" then let H = F + 2127
If E\$ = "Islam" then let H = F + 626

For each of these cases, the lines specify the number of years between the time something happened in a given civilization, and when you might expect something analogous to happen in the West. They were arrived at, frankly, by picking prominent personalities from the histories of these societies who seemed to play roles similar to those of Caesar in Classical times. The climaxes of the careers of the four "Caesars" are therefore deemed to be contemporary. The identification of Alexander with Napoleon, of course, is the lynch-pin of the whole system. (China has a figure rather like Alexander, too.) The Western Caesar can be expected to live as long after Napoleon as Caesar did after Alexander. The rest is history.

Perspicacious readers will note that the algorithm lines do not take into account the fact there was no year zero. Thus, the assignment of all events that happened before the beginning of the Christian era to corresponding dates in the Western future is off by a year. At least.

Not a moment too soon, the computer screen cautions:

A note of warning.

Haven't there been detailed refutations of both Spengler and Toynbee since almost the time their works first appeared? Certainly both have been subjected to telling factual critiques by experts in the places and times of which the two historians take such an imperial overview. Toynbee was more susceptible to this kind of criticism, since he set out far more facts than Spengler. However, the chief argument usually raised against comparative history of this kind, and particularly as practiced by Spengler, is that it rests on an organic metaphor. Civilizations (tricky things to define in the first place) are said to "grow" and "mature" and "die." How this sort of poetic diction explains the way event "A" gave rise to "B" in any given civilization is necessarily mysterious; to ask "why does this happen?" of Spengler is to be answered, literally, "that's life."

Many worthy commentators have remarked that this is not an explanation at all. The explanations for real events in history, such as why General McClellan refused to advance against inferior forces during the Peninsular Campaign in the American Civil War, or why the New York Stock Exchange collapsed in October of 1929, lie in specific, causal relationships. The explanation for historical events is never some generality like "Magian Culture" or "It was Autumn in China," or even something like "class conflict" or "the next step in evolution." An explanation is who talked to whom, what resources were available and what techniques were known to make use of them. The outcome of many battles can be explained by nothing more mysterious than the weather. It is possible to do comparative history of different cultures and different times without waxing mystical. The Annales school in France, and the American historian, William McNeill (a great admirer of Toynbee, by the way), have long shown that a historical narrative can link China and Europe and India, say, over a period of centuries without departing from the types of proof that would satisfy a hardheaded, empirical sociologist. The generalizations such historians admit to are small, but well-founded, and they all deal with the description of the past, not the prediction of the future.

This is an old dispute, and not one that can be settled in the introduction to a video game. However, for whatever it may be worth, it does appear that the physics of the late twentieth century is turning against the view of causation on which this anti-organicist critique were based. The critics assumption seems to have been that the behaviors of complex systems (such as a society of millions of people) are determined by the fundamental elements of which the system is made. Thus, systems that are made out of fundamentally different stuff, or that operate under greatly different conditions (such as societies with widely different levels of technological development might be thought to do) ought to behave in radically different ways. Two very different human societies, therefore, ought not to have similar histories, or even analogous ones.

Though perhaps cited in too many unlikely contexts already, it does seem that chaos theory puts all this into question. We now know that the same patterns will show up in complex systems of wildly different composition, from the growth of algae in ponds to the behavior of the stock market. In a way, of course, this is nothing new: it's not a revelation to be told that the same basic market patterns governed "tulipmania" in 17th century Holland as brought about the fall of the "junk bond" market in the 1980s in the United States. Can similarly analogous patterns hold for the behavior of whole societies over the course of centuries? Maybe; let's see. Even if they do, however, the program moves on to wisely observe:

The output of Dr. Spengler's Temporal Analogizer should be taken in a purely heuristic sense.

The data lines entered into the computer were necessarily chosen within the limits of the author's own biases and level of historical sophistication. They lean heavily toward political and military events, simply because such things are easy to date to a single year or range of years. They disproportionately make use of dates from the Classical world because that information is most readily available in the United States in the early 1990s.

Further, they deprive the reader of one of the great excellences of The Decline of the West, the attempt to identify the special spirit of each civilization. From the earliest hymns of the Age of Faith to the abdication edict of the last emperor, there will be a certain continuing style in the way a culture and its civilization do things, a style which will infect its mathematics and politics, its music and its idea of money.

Some anthropologists have been greatly taken with this idea. Ruth Benedict's famous study of four small non-Western societies, Patterns of Culture, even uses some of Spengler's terminology. The Hopi people of the American southwest are said to possess an "Apollonian culture," that is, a society which supposedly values limits and clarity above all else. This use of the term Apollonian (derived from Nietzsche) is essentially Spengler's. Indeed, Spengler's characterization of the Classical world as Apollonian, with its mathematics of solid bodies, its politics based on the citizen-assembly which could be seen at a glance in the city agora, its high art of the human form, is one of the most compelling arguments in the Decline. It was because of his characterization of the West, however, that the program gives you this final warning:

Dr. Spengler's Temporal Analogizer should be kept out of the hands of gullible undergraduates, German revanchists and recovering Logical Positivists.

According to Spengler, the West is a "Faustian" civilization. Readers will recall that Faust was a legendary Renaissance scholar-magician who sold his soul to the devil in return for knowledge and power. To be Faustian is to be impatient of limits, to seek the hidden, to take terrible risks. Benedict identified certain Indians of the American northwest as Faustian. Their otherwise well-ordered lives centered around ceremonies which deliberately created the setting for some dreadful excess. The potlatch is supposed to be characteristic of this kind of society, the ultimate in conspicuous consumption, in which great men give away or destroy a fortune in goods or money in order to gain prestige. (Actually, profligate benefactions by the rich to the poor were also the stuff of Classical Greco-Roman politics; in Roman history, the practice was called "bread and circuses.") In one rite, a horrible anthropophagous god would possess the celebrant, and participants were in danger of losing flesh to his bites. These were not the excesses of indiscipline; the culture acknowledged the limits of normal behavior by deliberately transcending them. It was the same spirit which made them the only Amerindian people to develop ocean travel.

Spengler's Faustian West, of course, is a being of immensely vaster scale and subtlety. Its science quite literally seeks the infinite and its technology is contemptuous of the human scale. It alone developed a mathematics which can deal with invisible

14

forces, by means of which the West has probed the regions of the earth and of near space that have heretofore been closed not only to man, but to life itself. Its political and military power has stretched all around the world. In its Spring, it developed forms of Christianity to which all human beings were to be compelled to submit, while in its early Winter it dreamed of ideologies of reform and revolution which would end the need for further social change once and for all, everywhere in the world. Its art is music, just as the art of the Classical world was sculpture. Music is based on harmony, the invisible force which operates between notes, and mathematical time, the clockwork of the Faustian soul.

This, at least, is how Spengler looked at his own culture. The description is cold, sinister, suggestive of limitless ruthlessness. Actually, this kind of deliberate self-diabolization is one of the recurrent themes of Western history. It is scarcely merited. The West was the only major civilized society to abolish slavery, or to develop the eccentric, St. Francis-like interest in the well-being of the natural world which stands behind all conservation efforts. Most claims by non-Western societies to have traditions of oneness with nature and equal respect for all human beings turn out on examination to be restatements of 19th century romanticism by local patriots. Even more curious, the West is the only major civilization to try to make a science of "getting inside the skin" of other societies. One of the most bizarre features of the world in the twentieth century is that there is no important critique of the West which is not of Western origin. As V.S. Naipaul once so cruelly put it: when you listen to Gandhi, you are not hearing ancient India, but Tolstoy with a bit of Ruskin.

Spengler himself realized that, while there was a streak of Viking ruthlessness throughout Western history, there is also a peculiar carefulness. Many societies have had comprehensive and draconian legal codes, designed to cover all aspects of life. What is typically Western is the idea of meticulous official planning of life with the intention of making everybody safe forever. Spengler identified this characteristic with "Prussianism," and maybe he had a point. Certainly the good, gray, Social Democrats who ruled Weimar Prussia carried on a tradition of community paternalism which may be necessary to operate any effective modern state.

Still, perhaps there is another dichotomy in the West more important than that between Social Democracy and the Viking Spirit. The archetype in the Western soul of the search for the ultimate was fixed long before Doktor Faustus had his shady dealings with the Evil One. The Quest for the Holy Grail requires all those qualities of deep thought and hard work which the search for mere power requires. The difference is, those who go on the Quest have the hope of becoming what human beings are supposed to be as the adventure proceeds, whereas Faust disintegrates as his power grows.

The characteristic enterprise of the West is not the war of conquest, but the Crusade. The peculiarly Western desire is not to dominate, which is common to many times and places; rather, it is the desire to be the instrument of universal redemption. The Crusaders have an ill-name in the Islamic world and the merits of the case cannot be decided here. However, though the Crusaders turned greedy and the sack of Jerusalem was an atrocity, the whole affair cannot be reduced to simple unprovoked aggression. It was sparked, after all, by a plea for help from the Byzantine Empire, which seemed to be about to expire in the face of a renewed Muslim offensive.

Consider how extraordinary a spectacle it was. In the early Crusades, at least, it meant that an appreciable portion of the governing class of a no-longer primitive civilization went on a

16

fantastic mission to the edge of the known world to rescue God (as represented by the holy places that were filled with His presence). Historical analogies are hard to come by.

This type of enterprise tells you as much about Western art and culture as it does about Western politics and military ambitions. The effrontery is breathtaking. And sometimes, as with International Style architecture or the music of Richard Wagner, it may express itself as the will to crush the audience. In its most corrupt form, it is the desire to shock and to destroy traditional sensibilities. The culture of the Weimar Republic was far more "Faustian" in this sense than that of its Nazi successor. Still, it is important to recognize that these things are corruptions, parodies of the spirit of the West.

Perhaps, one way to put it is that there is a quixotic, Celtic streak in the West which has been at least as important to it as Spengler's allegedly Germanic Faustianism. On good days, it is King Arthur who rules in the West (including Germany), not Doktor Faustus. C.S. Lewis once suggested something along these lines in his novel, That Hideous Strength:

"...something we may call Britain is always haunted by something we call Logres. Haven't you noticed that we are two countries? After every Arthur, a Modred; behind every Milton, a Cromwell...Is it any wonder they call us hypocrites?"

The future suggested by the commentary to the program is more Faustian than Arthurian. This is because it is easier to imagine modified forms of old evil than to conceive of new good. In this the commentary is certainly misleading; if good luck did not outbalance bad in the world, the human race would never have evolved.

And so, with that happy thought, we come to the final menu:

17

If you would like a survey for a particular year, please type '1' and press 'return.' If you would like a survey for a range of years, please type '2' and press 'return.' If you would like Dr. Spengler's Temporal Analogizer to tell you everything it knows, please type '3' and press 'return.'

Not without some trepidation, you pick option "3."

Antechronicles

"Mumble with authority."
--Steve Post Classical Music Radio Announcer

Note on the readout lines:

"Rome" signifies that the line deals with events in the Classical Mediterranean world, including both ancient Greece and Rome.

"Islam" signifies that the line deals with the Middle East, the Balkans and the eastern Mediterranean after the twelfth century A.D. The few applications of Islam outside this geographical region are self-explanatory.

"Egypt" and "China" are self-explanatory.

Note on Commentary usage:

The terms "West" and "Western" refer primarily to western and central Europe and the English-speaking world (especially the United States) from the late eighteenth century onwards.

The West is discussed in the past tense.

First Transition:

The Collapse of the Ancien Regime (1767-1830)

"We owe it to Napoleon (and not by any means to the French Revolution, which aimed at the 'brotherhood' of nations and a blooming universal exchange of hearts) that we now confront a succession of a few warlike centuries that have no parallel in history; in short, that we have entered the classical age of war..."

-- Friedrich Nietzsche
The Gay Science
1882

Readout

1767 A.D.
Egypt, 1780 B.C.: The powerless Thirteenth Dynasty begins, ending the classical "Middle Kingdom" phase of Egyptian history.
1796 A.D.
Rome, 331 B.C.: Alexander the Great defeats the King of Persia, Darius III.
1804 A.D.
Rome, 323 B.C.: Alexander the Great dies in Babylon. His empire is divided among his generals. The Hellenistic Age begins.
1811 A.D.
Rome, 316 B.C.: The cities of Greece regain their liberty from Macedonia.

1816 A.D.

Rome, 311 B.C.: The civil wars among Alexander's generals end. Macedonia goes to Cassender, Thrace to Lysimachus, Egypt to Ptolemy Soter and Asia to Antigonus.

1817 A.D.

China, 483 B.C.: Wu Tsu-hsue, a minister of the State of Wu who opposed its aggressive foreign policy, is ordered to kill himself.

1818 A.D.

China, 482 B.C.: Actual hegemony over the Chinese world passes to the upstart State of Wu, ruled by King Fu-Ch'ai.

1827 A.D.

China, 473 B.C.: The war-weakened State of Wu is destroyed. The Era of Hegemonies comes to an end. The Era of Contending States begins.

1830 A.D.

Islam, 1204: The Crusaders take Constantinople and establish the ephemeral Latin Empire.

Commentary

In each of the civilizations under consideration, the period previous to the one with which the program begins came in later years to be thought of as a Golden Age. Consider the list: the Middle Kingdom in Egypt, the Enlightenment in Europe, the Greece of Pericles and Socrates, and the "Spring and Autumn" era in China. (The Baghdad Caliphate in Islam still existed at the end of the transition period, and would do so for some decades more. Nobody said these lines would match perfectly.) It was the time of Kant and Confucius and Plato. This was the epoch when each civilization worked out all the main themes that would characterize it for the rest of its history. By the time the events indicated by the readout lines had occurred, each of the civilizations in question had matured. Each is already in principle what it later becomes in fact. In the First Transition, the civilization breaks out of its shell. It begins to address less and

21

less the demands of its own internal development and more and more the requirements of the "real world," or at any rate of the larger world in which it lives. The result, to all appearances, is a collapse or an explosion.

The collapse is most in evidence in Egypt, which was invaded during this period by the group of Asiatic peoples called the Hyskos. Something similar happened in Islam, where the old center of the culture in Constantinople was occupied by Crusaders and the new center in Baghdad was in the hands of incompetent adventurers. Meanwhile, waves of Turkish invaders increasingly dominated international life.

Explosions occurred where some great individual saw the possibility of taking political ambition to its logical extreme. In China and the West, this ambition was frustrated. The successful attempt by the king of the State of Wu to temporarily wrest hegemony over the international system from his erstwhile patron, the venerable State of Chin, resulted in the destruction of the upstart state within less than a generation. In the West, France was not destroyed by the excesses of Napoleon's ambitions, since it eventually recovered its position as the leading power of Europe, but it never regained the overwhelming predominance it had sometimes enjoyed in prior ages. Napoleon's achievement lay in demonstrating that, whether or not the ideas of the Enlightenment were true, there were certainly powerful.

The most successful of the transition tyrants was the Macedonian king, Alexander the Great. While Greek businessmen and Greek mercenaries preceded him by some generations into Asia Minor and Egypt, it was he who persuaded the unthinking of the superiority of Hellenic culture by the simple expedient of conquering all the surrounding civilizations. All three tyrants briefly controlled the homelands of their

22

cultures: Alexander alone among them laid the basis for the later colonial empires.

In this transition, practical life fell into chaos just as theory was approaching what it believed (falsely) to be the final truth about the organization of the universe and the nature of the good society. For almost three centuries to come, history is about trying to manhandle the facts of practice into the molds of theoretical truths.

Part I: Modern Times (1830-2061)

"...[O]ne passes to the realization that our own age is also a 'period,' and certainly has, like all periods, its own characteristic illusions."

--C.S. Lewis
 Surprised by Joy

Some civilizations have better modernities than others. Despite the often terrible nature of everyday life between the death of Alexander and the rise of Caesar, the Hellenistic Period of the ancient Mediterranean world is remembered as a time of brilliant philosophy and daring invention. As was the case in the later West, the international system was governed during its early phase by great colonial empires. At their centers lay great cities, where brilliant if irresponsible demagogues vied for the allegiance of the masses, while artists and natural philosophers competed to win the adherence of the educated to their creations. It is a time governed by the spirit of large, confused places like Alexandria or Chicago, rather than more human-scale communities like Athens or Florence.

At the opposite extreme, there was Egypt, where the whole episode is dismissed with the term "Hyskos Period," a time when that civilization was politically divided and produced no cultural accomplishments to speak of, or at any rate none that can be traced definitively to that time. It was only after its modernity ended that Egypt seems to have had the resources and leisure to produce the sort of anti-traditionalist cultural mutations that are characteristically "modern."

Even when literature and art leave a conspicuous mark, however, modernity everywhere is fundamentally a time when ever more brilliant people seem to produce less and less of

24

substance. As the period progresses, its art grows more and more-self-conscious until it disappears into technique. It is the time of Wagner rather than Bach in the West, of Legalism rather than the Mandate of Heaven in China. It is also the great age of reactionaries of all stripes, of traditionalists rather than tradition. Many modern political systems which are supposed to embody ancient principles are in fact faked antiques.

One of the remarkable aspects of modern times, considering the amount of energy and creativity expended during the period, is how little of its vast cultural output survives. Science survives since it takes up relatively little space (for better or worse: the facts of one civilization often don't stand up to examination by a later one). But the plastic and pictorial arts, the prose that critics come to blows over and the poetry that briefly seemed to change the world, all this is often known to later ages only through secondary sources. The originals may be destroyed or suppressed in the terrible final stages of the modern era. More often, they are simply lost or neglected as taste changes. As a rule, the more early-modern a thing is, the greater its hope of longevity. Works like those of Dickens survived (with occasional slumps and survivals), while almost none of the modernist Western canon was equipped to outlive the critical apparatus which called it into being. This is the era of experiments. In the nature of the case, they usually fail.

This also the secular age, the era when every culture produces its peculiar form of atheism. Take an example from a civilization outside the program. The Buddha, who lived during his culture's early modernity in the Indian scheme of things, as an "atheist," a materialist, one who thought that great world of matter and spirit could be reduced to the play of atoms. In the West, the millenarian antinomianism created by Karl Marx under the name of "dialectical materialism" served many people with the right education as a species of agnostic rationalism to the very end of Western civilization. Sometimes God is not denied but depersonalized, as in China and in esoteric Islam. The goal of each of these strategies is to so define the world that it is possible to "get a handle on it," to make it at least conceptually manageable. While the real powers of men grow during this period (new practical technology flourishes), people are all the more anxious to ensure that their metaphysical liabilities are lessened. In the modern era, the ideal cultured person is answerable to nothing and no one.

This is an era when the merely large scale of a project will commend it to even discerning minds. It is not the first period when this is the case, of course. In the youth of a culture, people were perfectly capable of making pyramids ever wider and cathedrals ever higher from sheer exuberance. However, one of the wonders of those constructions of the Spring is the sustained quality of detailed workmanship throughout. They are monuments with a conscience. They are big because the builders thought they were about something important. In the modern age, bigness becomes a good in itself. While the skyscrapers and amphitheaters of early winter may express the vanity of the magnate or official who commissioned them, these edifices bear no personal imprint from anyone but the designer: workmanship may maintain a high technical level, but it is no longer art. Artisans become workers.

Cities cease to be integrated communities, even in cultures where the city was the basic unit of politics. They grow ever larger, but some are more important than others, even in the Westernized world where communication between populous points became instantaneous within less than a lifetime after Napoleon. In any civilization, only a handful of population centers are world-cities. They are the places where the political

26

and cultural life of the increasingly ecumenical culture is conducted.

One of the things that grow most conspicuously, at least for the first half of modernity, is the size and ferocity of war. In Islam, most of the practical inventiveness characteristic of modern times went to the development of a wonderful military technique. That civilization almost overwhelmed the young West more than once, and its preponderance was not redressed until those techniques became in turn the basis for the drill and organization of later Western armies.

In China, modernity was called the Era of Contending States. During this terrible period, more and more of the human and economic resources of the Chinese world system were devoted either to conquest or defense, as the great powers one by one knocked each other out, guided by the dictates of new, ruthless ideologies. Of course, terrible wars within a civilization are possible at any time, and annihilating invasions from without have been an ever-present possibility since the beginning of settled life. Still, it is only in this epoch that the forms and limits normal to warfare among people of the same culture completely break down. Alliances occur, but the goal of peace through a permanent balance of power, or simply of a world composed of a multitude of permanently and equally sovereign states, is a chimera.

The world becomes divided into armed camps, and one side effectively wins long before the period is over. This, however, is only the beginning of sorrows. Collecting the prize, establishing a durable world hegemony, is sometimes the most dreadful thing that happens in a civilization's life. It is inaccurate to say that one state conquers the world by the end of the period, though in each case (with the possible exception of tiny Egypt), some state or people acts as a center of "nucleation" for the post-national world which follows modernity. Those nucleating states, such as the ancient Chinese kingdom of Ch'in, which interpret their destiny as one of world conquest, do not long survive their victory, as we will see.

In many ways, this is an era of fear, of loss of character. Such is the muddle that politics and statecraft become that, by the very end of the period, simple decisiveness is enough to bring the world into line. Throughout it, people live from one dread to another. They fear proscription by the resurgent patrician party, or social revolution, or disorder in the cosmos from human wickedness, or the Turks, or the greenhouse effect. Modernity might well be called The Age of Fear. When people cease to be afraid, as they eventually do, they cease to be modern.

Section One: Clearing the Ground (1830-1863)

"I had as yet no notion that life every now and then becomes literature--not for long, of course, but long enough to be what we best remember, and often enough so that what we eventually come to mean by life are those moments when life, instead of going sideways, backwards, forward, or nowhere at all, lines out straight, tense and inevitable, with a complication, climax and, given some luck, a purgation, as if life had been made and not happened."

-- Norman Maclean
  USFS 1919: The Ranger, the Cook, and a Hole in the Sky

Readout

1832 A.D.
Rome, 295 B.C.: Rome conquers the Etruscans.
1838 A.D.
Rome, 289 B.C.: Rome is defeated by the Senores, a Gaulish tribe, at Arretium.
1840 A.D.
Rome, 287 B.C.: A coup in Macedonia.
1844 A.D.
Rome, 283 B.C.: Rome conquers Corsica.
1847 A.D.
Rome, 280 B.C.: King Pyrrhus of Epirus defeats the Romans in alliance with the Greek cities of southern Italy, but is eventually forced to withdraw.
1852 A.D.
Rome 275 B.C.: Gauls invading Asia Minor defeated by Antiochus I of Syria.
1855 A.D.
Rome, 272 B.C.: Rome conquers central and southern Italy.

1862 A.D.
Islam, 1236 A.D.: The Arabs lose Cordoba to Castile.

Commentary

In all of modernity, this period is the one in which the fewest striking events seem to happen. It is as if the world during these decades were the tenuous atmosphere of a low gravity planet: the lack of pressure may permit winds of great velocity, but they lack the force to change much. The First Transition accompanying the end of the ancien regime seems to have exhausted all the capacity for dramatic action which civilization had in it. To judge simply from a chronology of the events of this time, it is a period of incremental achievements, of small wars for limited objectives, an international system with a plurality of roughly equal states or peoples in stable configurations. It seems, in fact, to be a return to the conditions of the previous century, but without the conditions for eventual calamity which existed then.

This perception is an illusion. The restraints on society and international relations which made the ancient regime what it was are gone: internal politics are no longer confined to certain families and carried out in cabinet rooms and harems, international politics is no longer restrained by traditional alliances and objectives, or even by the traditional geographical limits of civilization. This is the epoch of incipient democracy (in its various forms) and of the growth of the state around which the future universal empire will form. It is also the period in which certain neighboring barbarians, attracted by civilization's growing prosperity, become increasingly frisky.

Democracy, of course, is everywhere culture-specific. In the West and during Classical times, it was associated with the franchise, but even in those cases the similarities are more apparent than real. In the Greco-Roman world, voting rights seem originally to have been an incident of membership in the militia. In the West, they were originally a perk for property taxpayers. Thus, the female franchise followed naturally after the enactment of property reform laws which allowed married women to possess their own property.

Elections and democracy have never been synonymous. In earlier Greek times, lotteries rather than elections were regarded as the most democratic procedure for selecting an official. Voting for a magistrate, particularly in open assembly, was regarded with suspicion by the common people, because open elections meant the rich and eminent had a much greater chance of achieving office. Elections did not become identified as a democratic institution until parties developed which claimed to represent the popular interest. In the West, too, the democratic era did not really dawn until the candidates for office ceased to necessarily be members of the traditional ruling families and groups. The question is not whether the president is elected by the popular vote, the question is whether just anybody can be elected president.

This process whereby "just anyone" can become an important government official is something that begins to happen with increasing frequency during this period in all civilizations. The apex of the process is as likely to be a theoretically meritocratic civil service system as a universal franchise. Everywhere, it takes the form of an increase in the prestige of the military and the opening of its leadership to talents. The gradual militarization of society does not usually express itself in military coups and the seizure of power by the army, not yet. Rather, it is a matter of the state being increasingly structured along military lines. The aristocratic governments of the previous periods were hardly pacific, but their wars were in their families' interest (not their class interest: that phantasm haunts only modernity). In this early modern period, on the other hand, even when the personnel of important government departments still consist disproportionately of the members of the old aristocracy, the military and strategic policy of the state has a logic of its own. The state does not serve the interests of a certain class: it conscripts all classes to serve its interests.

This is the period in which the great revolutionary philosophies have their beginning, though they only achieve their final form in the last phase of the civilization's life. The result is never quite what their originators expect. Mo-ti's (Meh-ti's) socialism was by intent a theory of populist pacifism, not the heady millenarian brew that came out of the assimilation of his ideas into demotic Taoism. (We will have occasion to consider the fate of the statist doctrine of Legalism, produced by the scholars of the Ch'i Gate, at several points below.) Marx's theory of revolution was intended as a fairly straightforward program for the traditional European left to act upon during the next industrial depression; he could not have foreseen its catastrophic fusion with popular Christian apocalyptic. Even in those cultures which developed little of no theory of the downtrodden, the fact of class politics, riot and occasional economic civil war increasingly darkened the worldview of educated dwellers in the great cities.

Meanwhile, on the periphery of the known world, a political and cultural system is growing which will first begin to dominate civilization in the following century, and whose influence will be decisive even through the Imperial period to come. It is only on the borderlands, on the frontiers of a civilization, that it is usually possible for a new country to expand without being hampered by old, experienced neighbors, and to try out new modes of economic and military organization. At the centers of civilization, at Athens and the State of Ch'i and Baghdad, these events on the periphery are often scarcely noted. Indeed, the inroads of the nearer barbarians, which occur in more than one culture at this time, may seem more threatening to the traditional state of things than the antics of uncouth provincials at the edge of the civilized world. The coming challengers grow almost clandestinely, though everything they do is done in the plain light of day with no effort to mask their ambitions. For that matter, at this stage, they may have no particular ambitions.

In Islam, the new Turkic nationality was only gradually being formed in the vacuum left in Asia Minor by the decay of the Byzantine Empire. It is these peripheral powers, however inchoate they may yet be, whose energies are directed during this period away from the old centers of civilization and into the hinterlands. Nucleating nations tend to be frontier settler states. This investment of effort will prove decisive in another two generations.

While it is true that this is a period in which civilized influence continues to spread, and some states do expand rapidly and without great opposition, it is not one in which the civilized powers necessarily have all things their own way. The barbarian groups which cluster around every civilized society are quite capable of humiliating, and even nearly destroying, the forces of the mature civilized states. In some instances, even neighboring civilizations are a danger, as the case of Islam and the West demonstrated time and time again. The states of the periphery are still underpopulated and imperfectly organized, while the more advanced powers in the heartlands of civilization are increasingly taken up with populist (or at least anti-aristocratic) politics. The attention of thinking people is often directed toward inessentials during this period.

Section Two: The Decisive Lifetime (1863-1940)

"I welcome all signs that a more virile, warlike age is about to begin, which will restore honor to courage above all. For this age shall prepare the way for one yet higher, and it shall gather the strength that this higher age will require someday--the age that will carry heroism into the search for knowledge and that will wage wars for the sake of ideas and their consequences."

--*Friedrich Nietzsche*
  The Gay Science
  1882

Readout

1863 A.D.
Rome, 264 B.C.: The First Punic War begins between Rome and Carthage.
1870 A.D.
Islam, 1244 A.D.: Jerusalem is taken by the Egyptian Kwarazami.
1871 A.D.
Rome, 256 B.C.: The Roman fleet defeats the Carthaginians at Ecnomus.
1872 A.D.
Rome, 255 B.C.: Araces founds the Kingdom of Parthia, creating a threat from the east that lasts into imperial times.
1875 A.D.
Islam, 1249 A.D.: Louis IX (Saint Louis) leads the Seventh Crusade to Muslim Egypt.
China, 425 B.C.: The organization of western China by the State of Ch'in is delayed by a series of regencies for child kings.
1876 A.D.
Islam, 1250 A.D.: Louis IX is captured by the Saracens.

1884 A.D.

Islam, 1258 A.D.: The Mongols sack Baghdad. The Abbasid Caliphate ends.

1886 A.D.

Rome, 241 B.C.: Hamilcar Barca makes peace with Rome: end of the First Punic War.

1887 A.D.

Islam, 1261 A.D.: Michael VIII Palaeologus retakes Constantinople and restores the Byzantine Empire.

Islam, 1261 A.D.: Mamelukes conquer Acre, ending the era of the Crusades.

1889 A.D.

Rome, 238 B.C.: Carthage begins the conquest of Spain.

1891 A.D.

Rome, 236 B.C.: War between Sparta and the Achaen League.

1897 A.D.

China, 403 B.C.: The surviving Great Powers are Ch'in, Ch'u, Ch'i and Yueh.

1905 A.D.

China, 395 B.C.: King Tao of the semi-barbarous State of Ch'u attempts systematic internal reforms.

1911 A.D.

Rome, 216 B.C.: In a Second Punic War, Hannibal of Carthage defeats the Romans in Italy at Cannae.

1913 A.D.

China, 387 B.C.: Eastern China is gradually organized into a traditional league of princes under Ch'i.

China, 387 B.C.: Count Hsien ascends the throne of Ch'in and revolutionizes the country in a 24 year reign.

1914 A.D.

Rome, 213 B.C.: Rome conquers and sacks Syracuse, killing Archimedes in the process.

Islam, 1288 A.D.: Birth of Osman I, founder of the Ottoman State.

1925 A.D.

Rome, 202 B.C.: Scipio Africanus defeats Hannibal at Zama.

1926 A.D.

Rome. 201 B.C.: The Second Punic War ends.

1927 A.D.

Egypt, 1620 B.C.: Rule by Khyan the Hyskos.

1930 A.D.

Rome, 197 B.C. Romans defeat the Macedonians.

1933 A.D.

China, 367 B.C.: The nominal Chou emperor loses all vestiges of actual power.

1935 A.D.

Rome, 192 B.C.: Antiochus III of Syria lands in Greece.

1936 A.D.

Rome. 191 B.C.: Antiochus III defeated by the Romans at Thermopylae.

1937 A.D.

Rome, 190 B.C. Antiochus III defeated by the Romans at Magnesia.

1939 A.D.

China, 361 B.C.: Yang of Wei, minister to Count Hsien, reforms Ch'in according to the fascist doctrines of Legalism.

China 361 B.C.: The State of Ch'in expands west and south as traditional barbarian enemies are defeated.

1940 A.D.

China, 360 B.C.: The small states at the center of the world are gradually absorbed by the Great Powers, thus bringing the latter into collision.

Commentary

In this span of time, perhaps eighty years, civilization assumes the configurations which will be decisive for its whole future. These critical elements are not always those which seem important at the time. The barbarian hinterland of civilized societies, energized by social and technological advances occurring at the core, frequently intrude into wide areas of the civilized world, sometimes penetrating even the heartlands.

However, whether the barbarians are semisavages, like the Mongols in comparison with Islam, or simply younger cultures, like the Russians in comparison with the West, their impact turns out to be ephemeral. This, however, is rarely apparent as the cities they sack go up in smoke.

In any event, despite these incursions, the significant events of this period are often wholly of domestic manufacture. This is the period in which the many culture-specific forms of socialism, of the economy in the service of the state, become general throughout the civilized world. This, of course, means socialism in practice, as distinguished from the theories of social harmony produced in the prior epoch. All socialism is national socialism. It is the continuation in peacetime of those measures heretofore taken only in extreme military emergencies to control the economy and police society. In less technologically proficient cultures than the West, this can result in the creation of "nations" that are little more than fighting machines. (The percentage of the population which can actually serve in the forces of an industrialized society is limited by the need to keep all the factories running, even during a short campaign.) In all cases, however, it means large state enterprises, the attempt to maintain civilian morale by coercive measures, and long periods of universal military conscription for males.

Throughout the civilized world in the first half of this period we see nations pulling themselves together. In China and Rome, this is largely a matter of larger states absorbing neighboring statelets. In the West, there are the unification wars in Germany, Italy and the United States. In some ways, this process is more freighted with fateful consequences than the conflicts which occur between great nations. A state like Ch'in, with vast semi-settled areas for pioneering but whose centers of power are almost inaccessible to other nations, is in a far better position to expand its influence during the struggles that end this period than is a state like Prussia, whose new empire was an already highly developed region at the heart of civilization, but which for that reason was inevitably strategically vulnerable. As in Egypt, the process of unification may be almost invisible, but it is certainly going on.

Curiously, while terrible civil wars may occur during this period, it does not always occasion world wars. In Islam and even in China, it involved a long period of almost continuous pressure by the nucleating nations, the Ottoman Turks and Ch'in, respectively. Possibly because this pressure was always finding a ready outlet, there were no signal conflagrations, like the Second Punic War in Classical times or the first two world wars of the West, when it seemed that whole regions of the world had been permanently laid to ruin. The technological impact of the wars which occur during this period is probably important everywhere, but since not all societies conceive of technology as having a history, not all emphasize it in their records. Sometimes this spurt of ingenuity produces astounding examples of technological innovation which have no sequel. For instance, the only use of directed energy weapons in all of history, before the later phases of the West, was at the siege of Syracuse, when Archimedes used a concave mirror array to focus sunlight and destroy Roman ships in the harbor. This is one of those periods when practice easily pulls ahead of theory. Sometimes, indeed, theory never follows.

Still, those civilizations that have a penchant for social philosophy develop fearsome ideologies to justify these dreadful goings on. Some nucleating nations, like Rome and the Turks, get no further than a complacent nationalism, a manifest destiny, whose content is little more than the belief that universal domination just happens to be what they are good at, the way that some people are good at the plastic arts. Others, such as China and the West, make a conscious effort to cut themselves off from their own traditions of statecraft and morality, both personal and private.

Machiavellian political philosophies can be found in all ages, and where theoretical justifications of this type are lacking, the rulers are still capable of outraging traditional ideas of right and wrong without them. What is significant about this period is that ideologies to justify ruthless action are not just widely accepted, they are made into state religions. Scientistic ontologies will be created to show why it is right for the Party or the dynasty to have its way with its enemies without let or hindrance, indeed to prove that the authorities' cruelty is based on the very nature of things.

Political antinomianism is only a special case of a more general skepticism. This is one of the few periods in which it is safe to be an atheist (which in some cultures, of course, may take bizarre forms, such as astrological fatalism in Islam). Atheism is the natural companion of reductionism, the project of turning the world into a closed system. It is, perhaps, easiest to see this goal in ideologies like psychological behaviorism. However, the project is the same whether the world is reduced to atoms in the void or the alchemical elements. The point is to subject all things to the wisdom of the present generation, the first to achieve this bracing clarity of vision. The ideas of the ancestors, both for good and ill, seem to be entirely irrelevant to the present crisis (whatever the crisis may be).

The irony is that this great skeptical enterprise is made possible only by the vast reservoir of loyalty and goodwill which still exists in society as a whole, including most of the educated. This is also one of the few periods in history where family counts for less than patriotism in the consciences even of

40

ordinary people. At almost no other time in a civilization's life is there such a high percentage of "good citizens," paying their taxes, fighting in the wars, and generally crediting their rulers with a degree of competence and good faith rarely encountered among human beings they actually know.

To some extent, this is also the last age of great men. In any society, people tend to conform to cultural stereotypes. When politicians are expected to be criminals and embezzlers, that is what they will tend to be, if only because people of character will fight shy of a political career. On the other hand, when heroes are still believed to be theoretically possible, that is what people anxious for a conspicuous role in public life will try to become. Often this has comical results, since the social ideals which would-be heroes try to embody are often falsified recollections of certain aspects of aristocratic behavior from the ancien regime. ("Gentlemen do not read each other's mail," said the Secretary of State as he refused to read the decrypted diplomatic cables from the Japanese Embassy before Pearl Harbor.) Sometimes the effects are less than comical, as when a cult of deliberate ruthlessness develops among persons of low origin who seek power and influence. In the West and in Classical times, there was even a cult of the artist, whereby industrious persons with an artistic bent could claim to be Great Men, simply on the basis of being in the business of creating cultural products.

Still, despite the proliferation of cheap imitation saviours, this is a period in which great decisions are often made by sound statesmen on the basis of traditional notions of justice and equity. While competence and even genius in public life will be available in the decades to come, this is the last period of modernity in which the world is not governed by a frivolous Realpolitik.

As the period progresses, the fundamental cynicism of its guiding spirits becomes more and more debilitating to the whole civilization. In the early years, mass wars can be conducted with great popular enthusiasm without any manipulation by the ruling groups; the rulers and the ruled are ideologically one. Later, however, intellectuals and political leaders increasingly think one thing and say another, so as not to undermine morale. The point is not increasing dishonesty, but that the worldview of sophisticated people has grown so grotesque that they rarely dare state their real motivations in public. They believe that only people such as themselves, who have the training to study policy questions deeply, can be expected to make sacrifices for the public good on the merits of a question. Since in this period even the most willfully shortsighted cultures, such as the Classical world, must make some attempt at grand strategy and think of the needs of future generations, the people must be increasingly enticed towards rather abstract goals with slogans and fear campaigns, with bogeymen and catchwords. As cynicism grows among the masses, the rulers become ever less certain of the spontaneous obedience of the people they rule. New levels of political policing and censorship become necessary, even of popular culture. This is a period in which there are often many great victories, and all of them turn sour.

Section Three: The Short, Twilight Struggle (1940-1992)

Once upon a time, a Crusader met a Saracen in battle. The Saracen struck the Crusader's neck, a blow which the good knight believed must have missed, since he felt none the worse in the immediate sequel. What was his surprise a few hours later, therefore, when he tugged at his forelock and his head came off.

--An Anecdote attributed to De Joinville.

Readout

1950 A.D.
China, 350 B.C.: Land reform, police travel permits, draconian criminal penalties are introduced.
1955 A.D.
Rome, 172 B.C.: War between Rome and Macedonia.
1958 A.D.
China, 342 B.C.: The ruler of Ch'in acquires the title of Hegemon.
1959 A.D.
Rome, 168 B.C.: Rome defeats Macedonia at Pydna.
Rome, 168 B.C.: Macedonia is placed under a Roman governor. Rome is increasingly seen as world hegemon.
1967 A.D.
Egypt, 1580 B.C.: Ka-mose the Hyskos.
1971 A.D.
China, 329 B.C.: Ch'u conquers and annexes Yueh.
1977 A.D.
Egypt, 1570 B.C.: Reign begins of Ah-mose I of Thebes. Native revival.
China, 323 B.C.: Ch'u and Ch'i, after years of conflict, sign a peace convention mediated by Ch'in.
1978 A.D.
Rome, 149 B.C.: Third Punic War begins.

1980 A.D.

Rome, 147 B.C.: Rome destroys Carthage and Corinth; Greece comes under Roman control.

Islam, 1354 A.D.: The Turks take Gallipoli.

1989 A.D.

China, 311 B.C.: Ch'u loses a critical strategic pass to Ch'in.

1992 A.D.

Islam, 1366 B.C.: The Turks make Adrianople their capital, thus dooming Constantinople.

Commentary

In each world, the final shape of things implicit in the outcome of the struggles of the preceding era becomes discernible to the naked eye by the end of this period. In Egypt, it was clear that the days of the Hyskos interlopers were numbered and that the Two Kingdoms would return to native control. In the West, the American-dominated "perpetual alliance" of the major powers of the northern temperate zone (feebly represented by the permanent members of the United Nations Security Council) began to function in something like its intended form. Rome was close to converting the international system into a system of unequal alliances and clientage, thus transforming international questions into matters of its own domestic politics. The State of Ch'in's long accumulating set of strategic advantages became suddenly decisive, as the last barriers to almost uninhibited access to the heartlands of civilization fell before it. In Islam, the long-dwindling fortunes of the Byzantine Empire finally reached a state of hopelessness: the Empire had not only lost its ancient patrimony in Asia Minor, its enemies marauded at will in the capital's very hinterland. This time, they were not going to go away.

In each world, too, the political and military facts of this period are modified not only by the particulars of strategy as they relate to each civilization's geography and technical competence, but also by each culture's general style, something which applies as much to international relations as it does to its arts or philosophy. In China, warfare was almost continuous. Nearly every year, the major powers would be in combat either against each other or one of their smaller neighbors. Nothing was left implicit in this culture's international life. Economic capacity which was developed for strategic reasons was used to fight actual wars, not as an implied threat. Alliances were formed not to prevent wars but to fight them. All the while, an intricate diplomatic dance was played out according to forms which went back to the beginnings of the international system in the early days of the Chou Dynasty. (That institution, the theoretical centerpiece of the civilized world's political life, had fallen into honored decay centuries before in a way strongly reminiscent of the Holy Roman Empire in the later West.) This system of conflict and negotiation, however, almost never had the effect of preventing the outbreak of hostilities; it existed to facilitate them, to direct what would otherwise have been a chaos of all-against-all into the rational forms required by state policy.

The contrast with the later West is instructive. Both these civilizations assumed that the world was governed by impersonal, order-creating forces. But whereas in China during this cycle of civilization these forces were always thought of as being closely bound up with particular material bodies, the West assumed the existence of wholly disembodied forces, working in empty space. Western statesmen (if not soldiers) flattered themselves with the belief that they did not have to fight a conflict to be able to predict its outcome. Thus, the most curious effect of the strategic planning for cataclysmic future wars which became a staple of Western statecraft was to dispense with the need for actual fighting. In China, on the other hand, it was tactical theory which emphasized the possibility of victory through symbolic manipulation, without the need for a literal clash of arms.

The irony, therefore, was that in many ways this period marked the beginning of a lessening of military tension for the West, in that war came to command less and less of the attention of civil society. (Much the same thing happened in Classical civilization, where the most severe international conflicts of its history had already occurred.) Military forces could be large, but only at the very end of the modern period would they again be composed of conscripted civilians. The paradox is that even in the West, the number and intensity of military engagements began to rise. The lack of major strategic opponents made the possible consequences of small wars less costly.

Within the boundaries of the West, this period was entirely peaceful, continuing the style of statecraft invented at the beginning of the modern era. In this world, the exchange of information was seen to be as important as physical events. Where other civilizations might enter into half a generation of warfare to confirm the implications of a balance of forces which was apparent to all intelligent observers at the beginning, Western nations simply exchanged notes. Where victory in other civilizations meant the annexation of enemy territories or even the annihilation of other states, for the West the price of defeat in even the most terrible war might be no more than the co-optation of the hostile powers into international advisory councils and bureaucratic structures. However, while in principle these international bodies served the interests of the permanent alliance of which the United States was the lynchpin, they did tend to take on a life of their own.

Though in many ways the international system of the Classical Mediterranean was more primitive than either that of pre-Han China or of the later West, it did resemble the later

Western international system in that so much of it consisted of alien societies. The rulers of almost all the states with which Rome had to deal had Hellenic educations, they read the Greek classics and conducted much of their official business according to Greek models. Only a step or two below the aristocracy, however, traditional forms of life and thought went on with only the most superficial influence from the dominant civilization. This meant that the Romans often communicated at cross-purposes with the people they were attempting to bring within their system. While Roman domestic politics was intensely personal, the state was impersonal, numinous, embodied only by the assembly of the citizens. The Republic was based on the rejection of sacred kingship. Even dictatorship, when it occurred, was a constitutional office. All citizens recognized that the state had interests and purposes beyond those of its ephemeral rulers. Thus, repeatedly, the Romans found themselves at loggerheads with states whose submission they thought they had secured. In fact, the people in question thought that they had only been required to offer transitory tribute. When a neighboring king died, those whom he had overawed would generally feel themselves freed from any obligation to remain in submission to his successors. The tendency to regard the Republic as just another ephemeral sovereign caused no end of grief.

In many ways, in fact, this was the period in which Alexander's legacy seemed to be unraveling. The Hellenistic empire of the Seleucidae in Syria showed itself quite incapable of suppressing the nativistic religious revolt in Judea, while Parthia threatened the whole region from the east. All of the post-Alexandrine monarchies were rapidly going native to one degree or another. While many aspects of Greek culture could be enjoyed in isolation from the matrix of Hellenistic municipal life, the Greek habits of open government were not among the things which transplanted easily.

In this period, some of the policies and strategies which will make the later world polity possible are devised and fixed in stone. This burst of creativity, however, happens towards the beginning of the period. In several civilizations, there were examples of tactical overreaching. Indeed, this lack of surefootedness is apparent not only among generals, but also among artists, politicians and philosophers. In China, the contending states bite off more than they can chew from each other: what seem to be final victories turn into routs when the victors attempt to hold new territory. In the West, the American attempt to employ the information-theory style of statecraft (developed for the nuclear standoff) to conventional conflicts resulted in defeats wherever it was tried. As a military analyst would later remark, "We would not have lost so many planes if their defenses had not been so primitive."

By the end of the period, however, none of these missteps can be shown to have significantly influenced the course of events. The state of the international system at the end of the period merely served to clarify the results of the previous, decisive phase of the civilization's history.

This is not to say, however, that even the nucleating nations are quite without problems by the time this epoch reaches its end. Indeed, the long years of close state control of everyday life, coupled with the personal disasters which Realpolitik imposed on ordinary people, have soured the internal society of much of the civilized world. In most of the world, in fact, this is a period of fundamentally enfeebled societies, nations which cannot be asked to do too much, whose rulers fear to spark revolts even when national independence demands sacrifices. What are called "nucleating nations" were, in fact, simply those which were still capable of conducting a foreign policy directed at the policing of the entire international system. However, a stratum of personal indiscipline and potential political anarchy underlies even the most imposing constitutional and economic edifices by the end of this epoch.

Section Four: Imperial Populism (1992-2022)

"Constitutions should be short and vague."

--Napoleon

Readout

1994 A.D.

Rome, 133 B.C.: The reformer Tiberias Gracchus is murdered at the instigation of the Senate.

1997 A.D.

Egypt, 1550 B.C.: The native princes of Thebes reestablish Egyptian power.

2001 A.D.

Islam, 1375 A.D.: The Mamelukes finish the conquest of Armenia.

2004 A.D.

Rome, 123 B.C.: Gaius Gracchus, another reformer and brother of Tiberius, is killed in a riot. His reforms are revoked.

China, 296 B.C.: Ch'i assembles a league of northern states against Ch'in.

2008 A.D.

China, 292 B.C.: Ch'u is crippled by the loss of more strategic territory to Ch'in.

2012 A.D. China, 288 B.C.: The kings of Ch'in and Ch'i assume the title of emperor, though world opinion soon makes them renounce it.

2015 A.D.

China, 285 B.C.: Ch'i suffers defeat by Ch'in and neighboring states.

2019 A.D.

Islam, 1393 A.D.: Bajazet, Emir of the Ottoman Turks, conquers Bulgaria.

2021 A.D.

China, 279 B.C.: Ch'i is reconstituted after a brief occupation, but is unable ever to lead the international system again.

2022 A.D.

Rome, 105 B.C.: Marius and Sulla defeat the North African king, Jugurtha, who had suborned the Senate.

Islam, 1396 A.D.: Bajazet defeats Sigismund of Hungary at Nicopolis.

China 278 B.C.: Ch'in briefly holds the capital of Ch'i.

Commentary

In the midst of any painful experience, there always comes a time when one first hopes that the worst is over. The dentist seems to be about to put away the drill, you suddenly reach a part of the cliff rich with handholds which seem to lead straight to the top. These expectations rarely turn out to be justified: the dentist has put down the drill to find a knife to cut the gum, the handholds are friable slate that lead to an overhang. Still, the delusion is a relief while it lasts, and in certain situations it may revive your enthusiasm sufficiently for you to make some real progress. In rather the same way, this period of history is characterized, not so much by the belief that all problems have been solved, but by the renewed hope that progress is possible. The world system is obviously still changing, indeed doing so at a faster rate than in the previous period. Still, it seems to be headed toward an acceptable condition, one that can be realized with no major disjunctures. Predictably, it is the very successes achieved under these misapprehensions which inspire the folly and carelessness that eventually require a later age of discipline.

In the earlier regions of modernity, imperial expansion had usually been accomplished with the enthusiastic support of the popular party. The military, especially in conjunction with conscription, had become one of the great equalizers of citizens.

51

More to the point, it permitted populist politicians to use the state to despoil the resources of the traditional aristocracy. During the annihilation wars and reforms of two generations ago, this connection had become far more tentative, since the enormous personal cost of a forward national strategy was eventually brought home to every family. In the previous generation, foreign adventure had become more of a cause of the patrician classes than otherwise. Distant wars for subtle objectives could still be mounted, but the enthusiasm of the people could be engaged, if at all, only by invoking xenophobic themes and justifying the operations with platitudes. The effect was to remove serious discussion of foreign policy questions from the public arena.

This political configuration changed quite dramatically during this period. The engine for the new expansion was precisely popular enthusiasm. This was made possible by the fact that, as had been true a century and a half before, most people did not have to be concerned with military affairs if they did not want to be. The adventures of armies could be followed with the sort of detached goodwill usually reserved for favorite local sports teams. Even more important, the material advantages of these activities, whether in the form of lots of cheap slaves or a lowered cost of consumer goods, tended to dampen principled objections.

Again, every civilization is unique, so that the proportion of economic advance to military conflict is different from example to example. In Islam and China, the military element predominated, though the command economy of Ch'in prospered mightily from that nation's string of ever easier military successes. In Egypt and the West, the expansion was far more economic. Indeed, aside from actual changes in military potential, the most significant feature of the period for the West was the return of the United States to almost the position of economic predominance which it had held after the Second World War. Egypt, as it recovered from the disaster of the Hyskos Period, dealt with the rest of the world in this phase of its history primarily through border skirmishes. Even so, it was quickly developing a system of trade and tribute to the south and east.

The West, on the other hand, developed a science of conducting short, annihilating, brushfire wars, designed to achieve clear and limited objectives. Ideally, these could be conducted anywhere in the world at a few days' notice. When conceived and implemented according to strict criteria, these efforts were invariably successful. Their purpose, at least in theory, was to regularize the environment for the new international economic system which came into effect among already developed countries. Though the point was not always fully appreciated at the time, this meant seeking to ensure, everywhere in the world, that minimum security of person and property which is necessary for the operation of a market economy. In practice, of course, the strict criteria for these police wars were often set aside for reasons of American domestic politics. Still, the general effect was to make foreign and domestic policy mutually reinforcing.

As tends to happen in any system involving positive feedback, tensions were building which would eventually make the new modus vivendi untenable. Though submerged for most of this period, the conflict between the "patricians" and "plebeians" experienced by mature civilizations sometimes flares up during this epoch. "Plebeians," of course, despite their self-designation and their propaganda, represent neither "the people" nor the national interest. "The people" in reality is simply an abstract image of the population, one that leaves out the peculiar characteristics and mutual hostilities found among actual human beings. In Rome, "the people" included persons who owned several slaves, and who were often richer than the ancient families of the senatorial class. Politicians of all stripes tended to also be financiers, usurers, and commodity speculators. There is, in fact, a strong link between democracy and money wherever they appear. The "people" are the new class, whether they are bureaucrats chosen by merit in the State of Ch'in, the "symbolic analysts" of the West, or resourceful military men of no background who appear everywhere.

As a rule, these groups can be kept in harmony, or at least in a state short of civil war, as long as prestige and material benefits are open to both kinds of people. There are exceptions, of course. The attempt by the Gracchi brothers of Rome to proscribe the persons and confiscate the goods of large sections of the senatorial class was the first whiff of the political chaos which eventually destroyed the Republic. This episode, however, represented the hightide of truly ideological politics. The Gracchi were, after all, regularly elected officials. Indeed, the elder brother organized what may have been the only truly representative election in Roman history. The demagogues which followed them, whatever offices they might hold, sought formless power as the leaders of mobs. Though "the people" usually win the struggle of modernity, principled popular government does not survive this period.

There are, after all, other things for ambitious people to think about. Conquered lands and foreign markets and the wonderful possibilities for arbitrage available at the center of the world have the effect of resigning people who otherwise would think little of each other to cooperate in one imperial adventure after another. Eventually, because the accessions of wealth and power promote change and opportunity, entrepreneurship becomes associated more with the popular party than otherwise.

As the international system, and the domestic system of the nucleating nation, move into the final stage, the social space which can be occupied by the most successful necessarily narrows. This is because, in a unified world, local success becomes devalued. Anyone can be rich, many people can be famous, but only one man can be king. By this time in a civilization's history, it begins to become apparent in just what this "kingship" might consist. In the West and China, it is in the nature of a revival of a tradition of immemorial unity. In the former, the primitive "universal state" was the Holy Roman Empire; in the latter, it was the early Chou Dynasty. Indeed, this period marks the first time since the beginning of modernity that anyone dared lay claim to the unoccupied throne, under whatever form of words. The claim is indignantly rejected by the whole world, but the prospect can never be withdrawn. Whether the universal monarch is thought of as the permanent president of a council of princes, or as the popular (new class) dictator of the nucleating state, or as the conductor of the concert of nations, the goal has become clear.

With the prize in view, it can become the object of conscious ambition. When policy is made from ambition rather than on the merits, mistakes are far more likely. Sometimes, there are mistakes about who the realistic contestants are. In China, the State of Ch'i organized a futile alliance to forestall the ambitions of Ch'in, as the European Community did in the later West. Both ended on a farcical note. More important is the decay of political discipline in the nucleating state. It is always an illusion to think that you can reach the top of a social structure by eliminating all your rivals in turn. Since such a structure is a pyramid of living bodies, one finds that eliminating its constituent members, even if only from public life, has the effect of destroying the pyramid, apex and all. However, this is rarely apparent at the time. In this epoch, in fact, domestic politics becomes what all believe to be a zero-sum game. Note that this occurs precisely at what seems to be the moment of maximum international security, because internal business need no longer be deferred in the face of a hostile world. In the next period, policies based on this misplaced confidence in the safety of the international system have predictable results.

Section Five: A Comedy of Errors (2022-2061)

"...All these schemes were debated without staff advice or consideration of detailed maps. There was no inquiry whether shipping was available, nor whether there were troops to spare...It was cheerfully assumed that great armadas could waft non-existent armies to the end of the earth in the twinkling of an eye."

--A.J.P. Taylor
  English History 1914-1945
  (On the Origins of the Dardenelles Campaign)

Readout

2027 A.D.
Rome, 100 B.C.: The birth of Julius Caesar.
Islam, 1401 A.D.: Timur from Central Asia conquers Damascus and Baghdad.
2028 A.D.
Islam, 1402 A.D.: Timur takes Bajazet prisoner after defeating him at Ankara.
2037 A.D.
Rome, 90 B.C. Civil war in Rome between the popular and patrician parties. Marius, the populist, is driven out.
2039 A.D.
Rome, 88 B.C.: Athens (and much of the rest of the eastern Mediterranean) rises against Roman rule. Beginning of wars against Mithridates VI of Pontus.
2040 A.D.
China, 260 B.C.: There is a complicated series of wars involving the states of Ch'in, Chao, Yen and Wei.
2045 A.D.
Rome, 82 B.C.: Sulla becomes dictator for life.

2048 A.D.
Rome, 79 B.C.: Sulla resigns.
2051 A.D.
China, 249 B.C.: Ch'in absorbs the last territories of the nominal emperor.
2056 A.D.
Rome, 71 B.C.: Slave revolt under Spartacus defeated by the general Pompey and the financier Crassus.
2061 A.D.
Egypt, 1486 B.C.: Queen Hat-shepsut conducts a policy of external restraint and internal improvement.

Commentary

The three characteristics of this period are disorder at home and embarrassment abroad, climaxed by a season of rigor. Indeed, the end of this phase in a civilization's evolution is often marked by a period of what might be called "realistic Fascism." A hundred years before, the reformation of social life in the interests of the state was driven by romantic notions of world renewal, a blissful conviction that old standards did not apply. The intent is revolutionary. At the end of this period, outwardly similar measures are taken. They are enforced by various authorities throughout the advanced world. This time, however, the intent behind them is purely and consciously conservative. Thinking people come to believe (or at any rate say) there is no realistic alternative to the traditional forms of society and culture as they were believed to have existed in the past. It comes to be an age of faked antiques.

Neither are all problems domestic. The unpleasant feature of hegemony is that eventually you have to exercise it. Obviously, this can be extremely awkward for nucleating nations like Rome, which have been devoting fewer resources and attention to foreign affairs in the face of increasing domestic conflict. But even the State of Ch'in, designed for continuous world war and motivated by an ideology envisioning the manifest destiny of universal dominion, came to find the necessity of actually having to subdue the small principalities at the heart of the world was more than it had bargained for. The matter required exertions which were more than pro forma. For that matter, the tendency of civilizations to regard the world as coterminous with their influence can, even at this period, be shown to be an illusion. Though the whole last half of modernity is an era devoted to finding new forms of order, disaster is always possible, sometimes from the inside, sometimes from the outside.

Of all the major civilizations, Islam seems at every point in its history to have had the least control over its barbarian hinterlands. Except in military tactics, it never developed a decisive technological edge over the less civilized societies which surrounded it. Even worse, its geographical position at the crossroads of Eurasia made it almost impossible to defend even in the best of circumstances. In this epoch, indeed, the nucleating Ottoman nation suffered a blow when a nightmarish invasion from Central Asia overran even its new homeland. (Rome would have suffered a similar fate, had not Marius the populist demagogue defeated a Gaulish horde which invaded northern Italy about this time.) At a later and less resilient period in its history, such a blow could easily have destroyed it. It is illustrative of the deterministic power of historical cycles, perhaps, that at this fairly early stage in their career, all the Ottomans had to do to regain their position was wait. The hordes of Timur were part of no larger story. They exploded across the ancient seats of Near Eastern civilization like a flood, but seem to have altered the course of history not a whit.

Rome, and to some extent the West, present the extreme opposite example of civilizations whose problems were largely self-caused. In both instances, democracy (in the different senses in which these civilizations defined it) reached the highest levels it ever would. Rome, of course, suffered civil war and social revolution in the sequel. The West, pursuing its own highly idiosyncratic notions of justice and equity, came close to achieving equality of result for all ethnic groups and both genders in the most visible stations of public life. The problem, however, is that any position or institution which is manipulated to this degree soon ceases to be a real center of initiative or influence. Leadership is a fundamentally mysterious quality, not one that can be apportioned out according to legal criteria.

Not, of course, that the nominal leaders of society and government were unwilling to try. In Rome and elsewhere, this was an era of the expropriation of the rich, including the imprisonment and execution of old senatorial families. Social classes are not organizations, and so they can never come to power. What can come to power are alliances of people of various income levels and ancestry in the name of one or another social class. In more than one civilization, "the people" come into their own for a few years during this period. The result is the death of the democratic ideal where it exists, and the hardening of hierarchical structures everywhere.

Healthy politics, or at any rate healthy political discourse, is never about power. To take an analogy from economics, any manufacturing company that acts as if it is in the business of making money, rather than in that of making its own product, is not going to make a lot of either in the long run. In much the same way, ideologues who make policy for the sake of power, rather than seeking to make good policy with the hope of receiving power as a natural consequence, will soon find themselves out of office, or worse. In the West during this period, some classes of foreign military engagement were "popular," a situation that left the decision-making authorities curiously vulnerable once they decided to get involved, since they quickly lost the ability to deal with the matter on the merits. In the case of the West, as distinguished from more labor-intensive societies, the natural consequences of relying on a small, precision-instrument military to police the world inevitably became apparent once it lost a major battle or was needed in two places at once.

The reaction (for once the proper word) to popular mismanagement of military affairs (and so of the economy, which was increasingly international and so terribly adverse to political risk) was thorough-going, frequently unjust, often bloody, and entirely successful. In Rome and the West, the paraphernalia of the authoritarian states of a century before, martial law and the concentration camp, first make their appearance in earnest. These new institutions created by the reactionaries are only extensions of initiatives made by their populist predecessors, and they do not actually stay in operation very long. However, the charm has been removed from the nucleating states. Their people have seen no historical corruption will be spared them.

This is the last hurrah of the old-fashioned secret police, the kind who want to stop people from thinking certain things, rather than just making sure they do what they are told. Politics is temporarily closed down as a working institution, though the constitutional forms are maintained. These, indeed, are revived and refurbished to an extraordinary degree. For a few years, however, the reality of government becomes an exercise in vendetta on the part of the conservative victors, a comedy of hypocrisy on that of the discredited populists. Offices at home are filled on the basis of "merit," meaning the merit of adherence to the conservative party. Or, rather, to the conservative leader.

Much, though not all, of the special legislation going back almost a hundred years which had been designed to reshape the constitution of society is now eliminated. This in fact makes little difference, since the legislation had always had consequences different from those intended, but the repeals mark the close of an era. Hereafter, until the end of modern times, politics really is just about power, and ideology consequently withers. For real power struggles, no analysis is needed.

Abroad, order and respect are restored, but in some cases that is all. In Egypt as in the West, the process of international integration was brought to a deliberate halt. Queen Hat-shepsut contrived to gain control of her ever more militant and expansionist government, seeing that giving free reign to her young male relatives in their designs on Asia was incompatible with the traditional values of Egyptian civilization. For a few years this enforced respite was possible, and for a few years there was a revival of old arts and old customs, an attempt to think with a smaller, clearer perspective. It cannot last, however, because people like Queen Hat-shepsut (and Sulla in Rome) are wrong. The traditional society she is trying to preserve ended two hundred and fifty years before; the traditionalists about her worship a chimera, a historical reconstruction made of elements from the culture of the Middle Kingdom period taken out of context. When even people of goodwill come to see this, there is nothing to prevent the world from collapsing into its final state.

Second Transition: Final Agony (2061-2080)

"Modernism is over. Call the cops."

--Tom Wolfe
  The Painted Word

Readout

2064 A.D.
Rome, 63 B.C.: Rome completes the conquest of Asia Minor and Syria.
Rome, 63 B.C.: Birth of Gaius, later the Emperor Augustus, perhaps the most successful man who ever lived.
2065 A.D.
Rome, 62 B.C.: The conspirator Cataline is defeated and killed.
2067 A.D.
Rome, 60 B.C.: Gaius Julius Caesar, the nephew of Marius, is elected consul.
2072 A.D.
China, 228 B.C.: Ch'in conquers Chao.
2073 A.D.
Islam, 1447 A.D.: Murad II of the Ottoman Turks is defeated by Scanderbeg, assuring independence for Afghanistan, India and Persia.
2074 A.D.
Rome, 53 B.C.: Crassus is defeated and killed by the Parthians.
Islam, 1448 A.D.: Murad II of the Ottomans defeats Janos Hunyadi at Kossovo, assuring Muslim control of the Balkans.

Islam, 1448 A.D.: Accession to power of Constantine XI
Palaeologus, the last Byzantine Emperor.

China, 226 B.C.: Ch'in conquers Wei.

China, 226 B.C.: Ch'in conquers Ch'i.

2075 A.D.

China, 225 B.C.: Ch'in annexes Wei.

2077 A.D.

Rome, 50 B.C.: Caesar finishes conquest of Gaul.

Islam, 1451 A.D.: Accession to power of Mohammed II of the
Ottoman Turks.

China, 223 B.C.: The State of Ch'u is destroyed.

2078 A.D.

Rome, 49 B.C.: Caesar crosses the Rubicon, beginning civil war
against Pompey.

2079 A.D.

Islam, 1453 A.D.: Mohammed II takes Constantinople,
establishing the universal Islamic state.

Egypt, 1468 B.C.: Thut-mose III kills or overthrows his aunt,
Queen Hat-shepsut, and begins systematic imperialism in Asia.

Egypt, 1468 B.C.: The Empire period of Egyptian history begins.
Thut-mose III wins the Battle of Armageddon.

China, 221 B.C.: King Chien of Ch'i surrenders with his army and
the world is united.

China, 221 B.C.: The King of Ch'in assumes the title "First
Emperor."

2080 A.D.

Rome, 47 B.C.: Pompey, having fled to Africa, is murdered at the
behest of the ministers of Cleopatra's brother Ptolemy Auletes,
her rival for the throne of Egypt.

Commentary

This is the epoch of the last world war. The victor is often
regarded in later years as the most terrible man in history, or as
the greatest hero who ever lived, the model for all future rulers.
In the case of Western civilization, whose universal state came to

include the whole human race and the whole planet, one or the other of these assessments was literally the truth.

This is the period when the final restraints are removed. The international system has been so damaged, partly by war and partly by the interdigitation of the societies which compose it, that it loses all resistance to consolidation. Domestic politics in all major powers have lost whatever restraint constitutional forms may once have provided. The extraordinary cynicism and viciousness of political life is ultimately debilitating. For a season, however, it provides a reservoir of available energy, of competent people willing to do literally anything which seems to suit their interests, which can be harnessed by the right man. Against this force, properly directed by a single will, there is nothing in the human world that can stand.

The stronger a civilization is in absolute terms, the more terrible these years are. For Egypt, the smallest and weakest of the great civilizations, the beginning of the Empire seems to have involved nothing more than a coup at home and the undertaking of a spectacularly successful raid into Asia. Islam, intrinsically stronger but weaker even than Egypt in comparison to its environment, actually failed to unite its whole culture area when its advance to the east was checked; the failure was never wholly made good thereafter. (It did, however, succeed in securing its barbarian hinterland in southeastern Europe.) The great event that signaled the end of modernity, the capture of the traditional world capital at Constantinople, was not an easy undertaking, but the conflict which accompanied it was not on the scale of a world war. The Byzantine Empire was long-since conquered in detail; the occupation of the capital was a matter of tactics rather than strategy.

At Rome there was a civil war that at least implicated the whole world, since the participants had nations for their clients and supporters. Perhaps the most interesting thing about this conflict was that it constituted final victory for the popular party. Unlike a generation before, however, this victory did not precipitate class war or mass executions. The new dictator, Caesar, was at pains to conciliate the hostile elements of the existing society, rather than to destroy them. The only setbacks to expansion were secondary. The most notable one was in the east, where a Roman invasion of Parthia had been attempted as much for domestic political reasons as for strategic ones. The period also saw the final absorption of the Republic's traditional Celtic enemies to the northwest and the acquisition of territories which would prove vital to the well-being of the future empire.

In China there was waking nightmare. The most ruthless state ruled by the most merciless regime in the civilization's history had followed a policy of aggression and intimidation for over a century. Now it paid off. All traditional morality could be said to have failed, to have been proven wrong, simply because those who attempted to abide by it were seen to have been defeated once and for all in this world. Despite desperate resistance, more than was ever shown by the Hellenistic cities against Rome, the states at the center of the civilized Chinese world fell in quick succession to Ch'in, until finally the last of its traditional Great Power opponents surrendered. The worst that could have happened did happen, in the view of the educated. The victory of evil appeared to be complete.

In the West there was civil war and international war, fanatical resistance and the implosion of ancient non-Western civilizations into civil chaos. Nuclear, chemical and (non-lethal) biological weapons were used again and again against civilian populations. Strategic ballistic missile defenses worked just well enough to leave the combatants sufficiently intact to conduct conventional warfare in the aftermath. Meanwhile, throughout the developed world, and particularly in America, there grew up a terrible exhilaration with the prospect that, at last, it would all be over. The day had finally come when all the bad people in the world, foreign and domestic, could finally be brought to justice. It was a great age for commissions of inquiry and international tribunals concerned with other people's malefactions.

Like the other great transitions in the life of a civilization, this cusp between modernity and empire is often experienced as a different kind of time. It is as if the eschatological horizon had been met. Throughout history, people say that, if we continue our present course, then in the long-run thus-and-so will happen. This is the era when the end of the long-run is reached. At this time, all ideologies, all theories of society, must perform or be considered refuted. The apparent refutation of traditional ethics and expectations, the apparent breakthrough beyond the system of good and evil, give the whole episode, almost a generation, an uncanny undertone. It is a time of desolating miracles, of dismay and wonder. The elements are seen to revolt, whether in fact or because people are attuned to the unexpected. The light of the sun is a different color, for a few years.

Not the least unsettling thing about this terrible chain of events is that nothing in particular seems to cause it. At the beginning of the period, all know that there is a great deal not right with the world, indeed that there are any number of accidents waiting to happen. The well-informed even know the outline of what the world would have to look like to make it a reasonably safe place to live; they have the sense to tremble at the jury-rigged state of things. Still, the event that turns these chronic worries into an all-engulfing flood is small out of all proportion to the result. A lost election, an assassination in a royal family, the renunciation of a minor treaty, any of these can put every important question in the world at stake, if the time is right.

This is not to say that this transition is a time of random or even meaningless violence. Nothing important can lack substance, and so the people of this time are driven by real hopes and fears. Their fears are produced by the sickening realization that a defeat which they and their ancestors had been fighting off for two and a half centuries, both at home and abroad, can no longer be held at bay. It will happen in their lifetime, to themselves. The mob will finally rule, the infidels will take the holy city, their inhuman enemies will occupy the ancient homelands of the brave and true.

Modernity was about the elimination of borders between societies and those institutions within them which intermediate between the subject and the sovereign. At its end, therefore, there is no place for losers to hide. For these few years, the private and the political have merged, so that one cannot simply withdraw and try to make a personal peace; there is no place of peace, either social or physical, to withdraw to.

This is also a season of hope. There is the fierce joy of the victors in the fact that they now can do all as they would. There is the more modest hope among society's passive but intelligent classes, the people who usually make things work at ground level, that at least rigorous reform will now be possible, that radical solutions can be tried and may even be necessary. Finally, most important for the future, there is the species of hope that can grow only after despair has achieved complete victory. It can have no public voice for decades yet, but it eventually outlives every civilization.

Modernity was in some ways a vast hallucination. For ten generations, it threw up terrifying shapes and aroused strange enthusiasms, all the while making promises of limitless power and knowledge. Then, almost suddenly, it was gone, as transient and inconsequent as a thunderstorm. It is only when the world of time seems to be collapsing, when all philosophy has refuted itself and the philosophers have taken to composing panegyrics for the victors, that the truth behind history can again become visible.

Part II: The Glorious Future (2080-2309)

"Lo, I am about to create new heavens and a new earth; the things of the past shall not be remembered or come to mind.

"Instead there shall always be rejoicing and happiness in what I create; for I create Jerusalem to be a joy and its people to be a delight; I will rejoice in Jerusalem and exult in my people."

--Isaiah 65:17, 18

Some societies have greater hopes for the future than others. In Egypt, it appears that one might do no more than hope for a period of renewal after a time of troubles. A pharaoh who wished to take advantage of this notion might call his reign the "Era of the Repeating of Births," literally the Renaissance. The classical Greco-Roman world remembered, or thought it remembered, that history had begun with a Golden Age. Therefore, at the beginning of the imperial period, the early emperors were flattered with the declaration that under their rule the Golden Age had returned to the earth. In China, it was always believed that history moved in great cycles, and that in certain periods it was possible for the T'ai P'ing to be established, the age of highest peace. Islam looked forward to the end of world history with the final victory of the Jihad against the unbelievers, followed by the uninterrupted reign of God.

In the West, of course, the Future had been the receding goal line towards which humanity had been running since the dawn of modernity. The race had begun since before the beginning of modernity, indeed, since the Future was only the secularized Millennium. It was the Third Kingdom prophesied by Joachim of Fiore in the twelfth century, the era of a thousand years when the Saints rule everywhere under the sun. It is a time when all social and international problems are solved, when prosperity is assured and continuous, when success follows success with no end in sight.

The surprising thing for the West was that it actually caught up with the Future. It lived in that glorious epoch for over two centuries. Its every dream came true. Serious war was abolished, epidemic disease wiped out, hunger banished everywhere. Racial and religious prejudices were forgotten in a truly ecumenical polity. Permanent colonies were established on other worlds, the whole surface of the Earth was accessible to any reasonably prosperous human being for a few days wages. This is the period when a civilization is both fulfilled and exhausted.

Not, of course, that there aren't some surprises. The future is ruled, or at least refereed, by an imperial government that in principle commands the allegiance of all mankind. Sometimes the emperor is a disciplinarian, sometimes insane, often a well-meaning chief bureaucrat. At least in theory, and occasionally in practice, he is selected by the free choice of an ecumenical College of Electors. There is no pretence of popular suffrage on the imperial level; this rarely convoked assembly of the Great and the Good represents not the people, but Greatness and Goodness. There is no more fitting way to select the suffering First Servant of Mankind, even if he is in fact (often) simply his predecessor's son or (sometimes) the designee of the military.

However, while many people are often eager to relieve the imperial incumbent of the burdens of office and take them on themselves, no one seriously argues that the office itself should be abandoned, or that there is any ethical alternative to the universal government. Indeed, people exert themselves to stay away from conventional politics, despite the fact that responsible local government is still possible, indeed urgently promoted by the central authorities.

The fact is, however, people refuse to vote if given any choice in the matter. If they are compelled, they will only confirm the decision of the nominating authorities. Indeed, most of the social and political rights acquired over the course of modernity are less and less exercised in the Future (just as the duties of citizenship are less and less required of citizens). "Politics" in the broader sense of meetings of locally important businessmen and bureaucrats continue, of course, so that parks and public institutions are still endowed by the civic-minded wealthy. However, to everyone's relief, the duty to "participate" in the affairs of the day, to fight in wars for freedom and justice and to take seriously the ideas of reformers or reactionaries, is no longer an integral part of citizenship. To pay taxes, and to obey the criminal law, are all that the imperial government asks. After a while, few local governments ask more.

In this age of final consequences, many activities which seemed evergreen finally come to an end. This is the period when science and mathematics are seen to be completed, when the basic truths of the world are reduced to a few volumes and taught in the schools. This is not because of laziness on the part of scholars or for lack of public funds, or even because of a cultural discouragement of natural curiosity. Indeed, there are many great descriptive naturalists in the Future. There are great technical universities, and the exploitation of the existing stock of physical theory by engineers goes from strength to strength for at least a century. Science and mathematics come to an end, except as historical bodies of knowledge, because there is nothing more to say. The culture's way of looking at the world has been exhausted.

The same is true of all the arts. Despite eruptions of libertinism among the ruling strata from time to time, the mood of the Future is generally one of increasing puritanism, of belief in decorum, of respect for form. As we noted in a previous age, in the Future much of the literature and representational art of the modern era is discarded, often because of its (sometimes imaginary) scatological content. This censorship, however, is only one aspect of a great work of criticism and redaction. The goal, sometimes merely implicit and occasionally even denied, is to produce a common language of thought and feeling and reference for the whole world for all time. The surprising thing about this kind of effort, whether in China or the West or elsewhere, is how often it succeeds.

In the Future, prosperity reaches the highest levels consistent with available technology. Those cultures which favor private enterprise for economic growth find business enterprises reaching unprecedented ranges of operation and levels of complexity. However, the old intensity of the modern era is gone. The imperial government determines how rich and how influential anyone can be. Sometimes, the rich, whether corporate or individual, are simply expropriated, or called upon to provide some voluntary but unavoidable public service. Finance is at any rate less important. Great stocks of uncommitted capital only appear when sellers have trouble reaching buyers and people in one market have difficulty operating in another. Pure capitalists are simple middlemen. In the Future, the political and economic balkanization of the world which made great financial institutions and financiers so very important for a few generations is greatly reduced. The economic growth that does occur is largely a function of the scope of operation which has become possible. It is nothing less than the whole civilized world in most cases, and sometimes a little more.

The growth of the economy increasingly parallels the growth of world population, and both get slower as the period progresses. This does not happen in all regions of the world or at the same pace where it does occur; it is most pronounced in the old centers of civilization. The fact is, however, that the general vitality of civilization tends to decline in the later Future, even if public health does not necessarily do so.

The Future is not necessarily a time of complete peace. In this period, all civilizations expand their borders (even inflexible Egypt subjected an ever wider hinterland to systematic tribute). Islam went ever deeper into Europe, taking the Near East and northern Africa at the same time. China pressed westward toward the center of Eurasia and south toward Indochina. Rome went north and into Britain, and only toward the end of the period did it move toward the east, where its long-term enemies lay. The Western imperium, on the other hand, which controlled the whole planet either directly or through unequal treaties, expressed the tendency to expand by moving into space. This enterprise was never quite as economic as it was hoped to be, and the actual movement of people and equipment to the Moon, Mars, Mercury and, in the most tragic case, Europa, was always an expense only the imperial government could bear. None of these settlements changed the course of Western history, though they often influenced it. On the other hand, in the real long-run, far beyond the Future, they may have been the only enterprises by any civilization which altered the destiny of the species. (This was particularly the case with the long-maintained project to alter the orbit of any considerable body in the solar system which might conceivably collide with the Earth someday, thereby removing the chief cause of the great biological die-offs which disfigure the geological record.) For most civilizations, however, this was the last epoch when expansion was an obvious good. It was certainly the last period when their societies were competent enough to accomplish it.

Even so, however, these great exercises of power were not such as to disturb the average citizen. The Golden Age had begun, and civilized mankind settled in to enjoy it.

Section One: At the Court of the Antichrist (2080-2098)

"We have compiled Quotations from Chairman Mao Tse-tung in order to help the broad masses learn Mao Tse-tung's thought more effectively. In organizing their study, units should select passages that are relevant to the situation, their tasks, the current thinking of their personnel, and the state of their work."

--Lin Piao
   From the Foreword to the Second Edition of Quotations from Chairman Mao Tse-tung
   (1966)

Readout

2080 A.D.
China, 220 B.C.: The First Emperor attempts to build a totalitarian state
2082 A.D.
Rome, 45 B.C.: Caesar is made dictator for life and adopts his nephew Gaius Octavius as his heir.
Islam, 1456 A.D.: The Turks take Athens but are held by the Hungarians at Belgrade.
2083 A.D.
Rome, 44 B.C.: Caesar is assassinated. His heir forms an alliance with Mark Anthony.
China, 213 B.C.: The ecumenical government attempts to make Legalism the world ideology.
China: 213 B.C.: Confucian texts are burned and scholars sent to concentration camps, where many die building the Great Wall.
2089 A.D.
Islam, 1463 A.D.: The Turks conquer Bosnia.

2090 A.D.

China, 210 B.C.: The First Emperor dies, but the fact is at first concealed.

2094 A.D.

China, 206 B.C.: The First Emperor's son is assassinated and the world quickly falls into chaos.

Rome, 31 B.C.: Octavius, now called Octavian and soon to be called Augustus, defeats Anthony and Cleopatra at the Battle of Actium. Augustus is emperor in fact.

China, 202 B.C.: Kao-tsu establishes the Han Dynasty, later known as the Former or Western Han Dynasty.

Commentary

The examples for this stage come mostly from Rome and China, whose political lives together contain most of the elements characteristic of the West (that is, electoral democracy and a long-term multistate foreign policy, plus an ideological approach to statecraft). Another example, from a civilization not covered by the program, would be India in the time of Chandragupta Maurya in the late third century B.C. He is another "contemporary" of Caesar, one whose rule over a newly unified India was regarded as extraordinarily harsh.

In all these examples, the whole civilized world is subject for a few years to the will of a man with a plan. This plan is often designed to make the world exactly what right thinking people had been saying for generations that it should not be, a world ruled by a popular monarchy or a dirigiste bureaucratic authority, or even simply a secular military government. While in point of fact many aspects of this period last throughout the whole imperial age, the first tyrant is recalled in later times as an extremist, the exponent of a style of government too intense to last.

History suggests that being caught in a world all of which is ruled by someone with strong notions of how to make it different, indeed often with fixed ideas about how to make everyone happy and good, is at best very unnerving. The only way to get out is by fleeing beyond the limits of civilization, sometimes to barbarian states or sometimes to the wilderness. Of course, the imperial government is sometimes willing to facilitate this process by forcibly exiling those of its opponents it would be inconvenient to kill to places so remote as to be scarcely mapped. This is the classic era of concentration camps. Sometimes these are killing grounds and sometimes they are luxurious little cities where the former rulers of independent states can be kept in closely-observed idleness. Many are vast public works projects whose primary purpose is to keep political prisoners doing something of which the government approves. The Great Wall of China (actually, the Ch'in defense works at the site of the later Great Wall) is the largest terrestrial example of this sort of enterprise, though of course it also served a necessary military function. On a relative basis, however, the excavation for Luna City was the most expensive such project in human history.

Because so much of this activity was conducted by the government, the first tyrant's administration necessarily has a certain communist cast. In any event, the damage done by the terminal wars and the fundamentally capricious nature of the young imperial government do not provide an attractive environment for private investment. Infrastructure and capital-intensive manufacturing become near government monopolies for some decades. This class of communism, however, is quite different from the populist, levelling variety which may have excited the intellectuals of mid-modernity. Even the slogans are different.

In every civilization in which the first tyrant appears, his regime is based on a cult of personality which may have precedents in history but which has no equal. It is all the more effective for being genuinely popular. The characteristics ascribed to the first tyrant need not all be pleasant. Some cultivated a reputation for cruelty, though this did little to prevent attempts at assassination. (This is also a great age of highly public and extremely ingenious methods of execution.) There is a kind of popularity which rests precisely on fear, enhanced by sometimes exaggerated ideas of the tyrant's competence and omniscience. The cults of certain ancient national gods, from Mexico to Carthage, were built on this fear. A populace that watches the hearts of a thousand victims torn out in the course of an afternoon may storm the temple to stop it or they may cheer; they cannot remain indifferent. Such a theocracy is supported by the solidarity which arises among people who see themselves as part of a system based on the public sacrifice of their fellow creatures. Similarly, the worship of great dictators is a way for the people to project their responsibility onto the top of the system. Far from creating loathing for the tyrant, the cruelty of his regime creates gratitude. For a few years, such a system constitutes the civil life of the whole world.

This was a hard time to be an intellectual of any description. Traditionalists, who taught that the past contained principles which limit what the executive elements of society might decide to do, were likely to find themselves digging tunnels, or out of job, or given the choice between evisceration and suicide. Realists and modernists, on the other hand, found that, although they were willing to endorse every government reform campaign and every rising minister, these occasions for the expression of loyalty tended to succeed each other so frequently as to make perfect fidelity impossible. Since such people necessarily made their professions of loyalty in public, this meant that they could always be branded traitors in a year or two, if the policy which excited their declarations was reversed. This frequently happened.

The first tyrant is usually a personally brave man, to begin with. His personality tends to decay with the course of time, because his victory means that there is no one in the world to give him a reality check. The great exception to the corruption of power was Caesar himself, who was always a generous and courageous person. Indeed, it was his insistence on mixing with the Senate as if he were simply another tribune which made it possible to assassinate him. In all other civilizations, leaders retreat into their bunkers and their harems, and even their closest advisers must speak to them on their knees or after an electronic scan for concealed weapons. There is no record that these measures have ever actually prevented assassination attempts, of course. This, and the fact that the first tyrant is never forewarned about the conspicuous miscarriage of his policies, induces first anger and then fear in the imperial incumbent. Indeed, in a world where everyone is a little afraid all the time and those in positions of power live in a state of intermittent terror, the origin of the great fear can be found at the very center, in the heart of the ruler of all mankind.

All the resources of a militant world civilization cannot keep a ruler breathing forever, and indeed the first tyrants are rarely very long-lived. These rulers, who were willing to leave nothing in the world to chance, also tried to ensure the continuation of their regimes through careful succession schemes. These often, though not inevitably, go spectacularly wrong. In China, the State of Ch'in which had relentlessly striven to unite the world over 250 years disintegrated in the civil war that followed the death of the First Emperor and his shortlived heir. In Rome, where matters went rather more as planned, there was still a sloppy and grotesque succession struggle, involving war both foreign and domestic, between Caesar's heir and other factions of the Roman ruling class. This conflict was not so terrible as those which led to world unification; it was not a world war, but a world civil war of the new type.

As is often the case when a civilization ages, echoes from its earlier phases can be sensed in these events, reversing the transformation that modernity had made in so many institutions. A world civil war is like an eighteenth century war in Europe, an affair of the rulers with no particular ideological content. Citizens must pay for it, but at least they are not normally expected to participate, and the war is almost never directed against civilians.

The victor in this case, however, is the savior of mankind. He is often also the most effective hypocrite in his civilization's history. Augustus proclaimed an age of peace and healing for the whole world, while executing all those ill-disposed persons whom his uncle Caesar had been willing to pardon. The founder of the Han Dynasty had pledged independence for the ancient states conquered by Ch'in and a return to traditional forms of government, while in fact consolidating the imperial power. The Emperor of the West justified his regime in part as the realization of the Christian Millennium, yet routinely used weapons of mass destruction against quite minor insurrections. In India, the Emperor Asoka, greatest hypocrite of them all, made Buddhism the world religion and compassion the chief slogan of a government which used one out of twenty of its subjects as a spy.

Still, considering human nature and the circumstances, these real "first emperors" constitute a genuine improvement on the disorders of the last generation, indeed on all of modernity. For the first time in centuries, government seeks to have only sufficient power to govern, not all the power it can get. The imperial period has begun, and the world can go back to something like normal history for many generations.

Section Two: The Early Empire (2098-2203)

"There never was an 'early Roman Empire.' It was always a late afternoon kind of thing."

--R.A. Lafferty
  Past Master
  (1968)

Readout

2102 A.D.
Egypt, 1445 B.C.: Cult of the athlete. Amen-hotep II has himself presented as a physical superman.
Egypt, 1445 B.C.: Religious syncretism and universalism. A new, disturbing realism in art.
2107 A.D.
Islam, 1481 A.D.: Death of Mohammed II. Accession of Sultan Bajazet II.
2110 A.D.
China, 190 B.C.: The Former Han Dynasty supports economic growth through government enterprise and an expansionist policy westward.
2118 A.D.
Rome, 9 B.C.: A Roman army penetrates to the Elbe.
Islam, 1492 A.D.: The Spanish complete the conquest of Muslim Spain.
Islam. 1492 A.D.: Bajazet II invades Hungary and defeats the Hungarians at the Save River.
2120 A.D.
Islam, 1494 A.D.: The birth of Suleiman the Magnificent.
2125 A.D.
Islam, 1499 A.D.: The Turks defeat the Venetian fleet; Lepanto surrenders.

2127 A.D.

Islam, 1501 A.D.: The Sheik of Ardabil, Ismail I, conquers Persia and establishes the Safavid Dynasty.

2137 A.D.

Rome, 9 A.D.: A Roman army is destroyed in the Teutoberger Forest.

2138 A.D.

Islam, 1512 A.D.: The death of Bajazet II.

2140 A.D.

Islam, 1514 A.D.: Sultan Selim I attacks Persia.

2141 A.D.

Rome, 14 A.D.: Augustus dies and is succeeded by Tiberius.

Islam, 1515 A.D.: Selim conquers eastern Anatolia and Kurdistan.

Egypt, 1406 B.C.: Beginning of the reign of Amen-hotep III, who violated tradition by marrying the common woman, Tiy.

Egypt, 1406 B.C.: The beginning of the obsession with the colossal in art. The Colossi of Memnon are built.

2142 A.D.

Islam, 1516 A.D.: Selim defeats the Muslim Egyptians and conquers Syria.

2143 A.D.

Islam, 1517 A.D.: The Turks take Cairo. The Two Holy Places fall under the Sultan's protection.

2146 A.D.

Islam, 1520 A.D.: Accession of Suleiman the Magnificent, during whose reign the empire reaches its greatest extent.

2147 A.D.

Islam, 1521 A.D.: Suleiman takes Belgrade.

2152 A.D.

Islam, 1526 A.D.: The Turks defeat the Hungarians at the catastrophic Battle of Mohacs.

2153 A.D.

Rome, 26 A.D.: Tiberius retires to Capri and becomes increasingly strange.

2155 A.D.
Islam, 1529 A.D.: The Turks lay siege to Vienna. The apogee of empire is reached. They are soon forced to withdraw.
2160 A.D.
China, 140 B.C.: Accession of Emperor Wu-ti, the "Marshall Emperor," under whom the empire reaches its greatest extent.
Islam, 1536 A.D.: Charles V, Holy Roman Emperor, conquers and briefly holds Tunis.
2163 A.D.
China, 137 B.C.: Sentiment grows that the government should rule more by example than force. State military and economic activities fall under suspicion.
2164 A.D.
Rome, 37 A.D.: Tiberius dies and is succeeded by the already strange Caligula.
China, 136 B.C.: Confucianism becomes the official philosophy of the Empire.
2167 A.D.
Islam, 1541 A.D.: Suleiman annexes Hungary.
2169 A.D.
Rome, 42 A.D.: Caligula is assassinated by the Praetorian Guard and succeeded by Claudius.
2170 A.D.
Rome, 43 A.D.: Rome begins colonization of Britain.
2172 A.D.
Egypt, 1375 B.C.: Amen-hotep IV comes to power, eventually changing his name to Akh-en-Aton.
2174 A.D.
Islam, 1548 A.D.: The Turks occupy the Persian city of Tabriz.
2178 A.D.
Egypt, 1369 B.C.: The former theological ideology of society is rejected. A new, universal, manifest god is proclaimed.
Egypt, 1369 B.C.: The Amarna Period begins. Old canons of art are rejected for experimental techniques.
Egypt, 1369 B.C.: Vast, uneconomic building projects are begun at home while the empire aboard threatens to collapse.

2185 A.D.

Rome, 58 A.D.: Nero comes to power through the intrigues of his mother, Agrippina.

2186 A.D.

Islam, 1560 A.D.: The Turks rout the Spanish Fleet off Tripoli.

2191 A.D.

Rome, 64 A.D.: First persecution of Christians.

2192 A.D.

Rome, 65 A.D.: Nero orders his chief minister and one-time tutor, the philosopher Seneca, to commit suicide.

Islam, 1566 A.D.: Death of Suleiman the Magnificent. Selim II becomes Sultan.

2195 A.D.

Rome, 68 A.D.: Nero is forced to commit suicide after a coup.

Rome, 68 A.D.: The emperors Galba, Otho and Vitellinus follow in quick succession.

Egypt, 1352 B.C. The Pharaoh's loathsome favorite and co-ruler, Smenk-ka-Re, comes to an untimely end. 2196 A.D.

Rome, 69 A.D.: The soldier emperor Vespasian comes to power.

2197 A.D.

Islam, 1571 A.D.: Don John of Austria defeats the Turkish fleet off Lepanto, ending the era of Turkish naval predominance.

2200 A.D.

Islam, 1574 A.D.: Murad III becomes Sultan.

China, 100 B.C.: The historian Ssu-ma Ch'ien writes the definitive history of ancient China.

2203 A.D.

Egypt, 1344 B.C.: A restoration of order and piety is attempted. However, the successor of the heretic ruler is assassinated. His name is Tut-ankh-Amon.

Commentary

A universal polity cannot be established in a day. For some generations into the imperial period, the empire has still to determine just what its constitutional arrangements will be, how large it can become, just what form of the civilization's traditional culture is to be promoted and which suppressed. This first fifth or so of the empire's history is full of incident, indeed some of the most colorful things that ever occur in any civilization's lifetime. It is, on the whole, a fundamentally prosperous period. The economy is still vigorously expanding, many technical ideas from the modern era have yet to be exploited fully, population growth is slowing but continuing.

It is a great age for attempts to revive traditional forms of piety, indeed for traditional usages generally. Old liturgical languages come back, as do archaic forms of dress for official occasions and ancient honorific titles. There is often a somewhat fancy-dress atmosphere to these exercises, however. People do them, not because they believe the theology or political theory behind them, or because they believe, as their ancestors did, that they are the right thing to do. They do them because they believe that these customs contribute to social order, or they simply enjoy them as kitsch. In fact, few of these anachronisms develop any great vitality; they are faddish for a few years and then are abandoned again. In terms of entertainment value, after all, they have to compete with popular culture and an unofficial "serious" culture which are still quite lively and maintain many modern features.

Indeed, even when the cultural policy of the Empire is traditionalist in intent, it is likely to mutate in quite new ways, for the simple reason that historical styles are cultivated with more enthusiasm than understanding. Official Egyptian policy after the Hyskos period, for instance, was obviously directed at restoring the integrity of the civilization's cultural and political life. Even so, the art of the early imperial period developed realistic touches which were quite unsettling to those familiar with the classic styles of the Middle Kingdom. More to the point, in all civilizations, the art of this period tends to become simply bigger. Gigantic statuary, planned cities with sweeping vistas, buildings that test the limits of contemporary engineering, these sprout up all over the world. At the domestic level, art becomes more and more derivative, even among the wealthy. It can still be skillful, even moving, but technique becomes ever more frozen. It is, perhaps, in the fine arts that innovation first ceases because all questions have been answered.

Here too, of course, there is a great deal of simple kitsch. During this period, for instance, there was a generation when Roman domestic architecture took on a decided Egyptianizing tendency, as did the fancy-religions patronized by the wealthy. Much the same happened in the Empire of the West in connection with the conventional art of the Far East (except, curiously enough, in the Far East itself, where Biedermeier decor experienced a last, ghastly revival). In general, however, decoration proceeds in too eclectic a manner to permit of regional or period characterization. Thus, while the cores of the twenty-second century cities contained buildings of a size which no other civilization could have managed, the interiors of these structures would have held few surprises for anyone born after 1950 A.D.

Several civilizations achieved their maximum territorial extent during this period, and none later acquired territory which they held for any length of time or developed to any purpose. Both Rome and Islam were checked in their attempts to expand into different parts of Europe. China's expansion seems to have been limited more by the logistics of supporting armies greatly distant from the heartland of civilization than by the military prowess of the barbarians. The same was true, on a smaller scale, of Egypt. Only Rome and the West attempted to colonize lands that were really new to their civilizations, the former by the effort to settle Britain, the latter by its long and only partially successful assault on the planets of the inner solar system (excluding Venus). The British project seemed to have been entirely successful, as did the lunar cities. The vitality of the smaller bases of the more distant planets, which were necessarily more self-supporting, appeared then and later to be more problematical.

One of the many questions which it is the function of the early empire to answer is, "Just how silly can the emperor be without causing the empire to collapse?" The answer, in every case, is "Very silly indeed." This formulation of the matter, of course, trivializes the experience of thousands of public servants whose careers, and occasionally whose lives, were at the mercy of a universal autocrat who might not always be in perfectly secure possession of his right mind. To limit this problem, some civilizations develop an office of censor or chief minister whose job it is precisely to police the excesses of Imperial enthusiasm. Some, like Rome, simply permitted the emperor to surround himself with thugs and secret police agents more dangerous to him than to the populace. Despite this, however, lunacy will out, and a universal state can sometimes give it a very broad stage.

Perhaps the most famous of these freaks was the Amarna period of Egyptian history, precisely contemporary with Nero's Rome. In neither of these episodes was the emperor actually insane. Clinically demented rulers who try to actually rule, such as Caligula, do not live long. In both the Egyptian and the Roman instances, we find examples of cranks raised to positions of supreme power. A crank is an otherwise sane person whose mind is dominated by some theory or ambition which does not really merit that much attention. There have been great cranks in history, and these two were among the greatest of them all.

The difference, of course, was that Nero merely embarrassed the imperial office with his pretensions as an actor, while Akh-en-Aton undermined the theocratic principle by trying to substitute his fancy religion for the traditional state cults. His essentially private cult of monotheistic sun worship is often discussed as if it were a great advance on the traditional religion of Egypt, and much ink has been spilt trying to connect it to the faith of the ancient Hebrews. In point of fact, Akh-en-Aton's religious universalism, of which he was the chief and only prophet, was as ersatz as anything a nineteenth century Western theosophist might have conceived. Not unconnected with his assault on traditional piety was his patronage of the anti-traditional elements in the art of the imperial period, the caricature-like realism which flew in the face of Egypt's hard-won standards of dignity and public virtue. No less serious than the consequences of these enthusiasms, he neglected the defense of the empire while squandering its wealth on a new show-city for which there was no particular need.

Indeed, compared to Akh-en-Aton's antics, Nero's reign was a model of sober good government. The Roman emperor, after all, conducted a reasonably successful foreign policy, and he did not actually bankrupt the state. As a rule, he was only dangerous to his relatives and his immediate subordinates. The exception to this was his initiation of the antichristian persecution, an eccentric element of Roman policy which yet persisted through most of the imperial period. Finally, it might be noted that there is some reason to believe that he was a better actor than Roman historians were willing to admit.

In any event, the early imperial period closes with a bit of a chill. If the military have dominated hitherto, the civilians point to the stresses which an expansionist policy has created and push for a policy of retrenchment. If the imperial administration has been largely civilian in nature, then it is time for soldier emperors to exert some discipline over the government and the barbarian environment of the empire. Even in Egypt, whose fragile Asiatic empire collapsed for several decades, this development is just a slight change of emphasis, one quite beyond the horizon of most imperial citizens. Indeed, most activities of "the Empire" have a certain abstract quality for most people. The Emperor, whoever he may be, is usually respected and often loved. However, he almost never comes to visit, and the doings of his government have little direct effect on everyday life.

Section Three: Apogee (2203-2244)

"Woe to the age that understands Tacitus."

--Proverb of German Historians

Readout

2205 A.D.
Egypt, 1342 B.C.: The reactionary general, Har-em-Hab, rules for 30 years. The empire is in disorder. Priority is given to restoring order at home.
2206 A.D.
Rome, 79 A.D.: Titus succeeds his father Vespasian.
2208 A.D.
Rome: 81 A.D.: Titus is succeeded by his cruel and paranoid son, Domitian.
2213 A.D.
China, 87 B.C.: Death of the Emperor Wu-ti.
2219 A.D.
China, 81 B.C.: The government debates the privatization of the salt, iron and spirits monopolies. Government control of the economy begins to loosen.
2221 A.D.
Islam, 1595 A.D.: The Turks defeat the Holy Roman army in northern Austria.
2223 A.D.
Rome, 96 A.D.: The competent emperor Nerva restores order.
2225 A.D.
Rome, 98 A.D.: The emperor Trajan ascends the throne. The empire achieves its greatest extent during his reign. Vast, underfunded building projects are begun throughout the empire.
2229 A.D.
Islam, 1603 A.D.: Ahmad I becomes Sultan.

2230 A.D. Islam, 1604 A.D.: The Persians take Tabriz from the Turks.

2239 A.D.

Islam, 1613 A.D.: The Turks invade Hungary.

2242 A.D.:

Egypt, 1305 B.C.: Ramses I establishes the Nineteenth Dynasty.

Egypt, 1305 B.C.: The bases of economic power shift to new regions. Theology takes an ecumenical twist, but within established traditions.

2244 A.D.:

Rome, 117 A.D.: The historian Tacitus writes an influential history of the imperial age.

Rome, 117 A.D.; The reign of the Emperor Hadrian is taken up with reducing Trajan's conquests to manageable proportions.

Egypt, 1303 B.C.: The empire reexpands under Seti I.

Commentary

This age is like one of those interminable story serials, familiar alike to readers of medieval romances and viewers of television soap operas, for which it makes no difference whether you skip episodes or go right through; the period makes as much sense either way. This is the deepest future, the closest any society ever comes to heaven on earth, the true T'ai P'ing. All problems have been solved, in the sense that all imaginable social and political catastrophes have already occurred. Workable precedents have been established for dealing with them for all time to come. The Titanic is built to be unsinkable.

Of course, human nature being what it is, there is still no end of people who are treated unjustly or who are oppressed, or who simply hate their lives. Societies that had always rested on slavery continue to do so in this period. Empires whose idea of international relations consists of exacting tribute under threat of punitive raids carry on in the same fashion. The best that a civilization can do is not necessarily very good. Whatever its ideals may be, however, this is the period in which the civilization comes closest to achieving them. It is therefore also the period in which the idea of fundamental social change finally dies out, at least as a serious secular possibility. The patricians and the people, or those who spoke for them, had fought for centuries about who would rule. The question now lapses, even in theoretical terms, for lack of interest.

Happiness is not to be confused with simple debility. For the last time, this period sees an imperial government capable of serious initiatives and a civil economic sector with the resources to support them. Indeed, the civil economy may show signs of renewed vigor and independence in this epoch, striking out in new directions on its own with only limited government supervision. The circumstances with which each civilization has to deal varies from case to case, of course. Nevertheless, all seem to achieve pretty much what they intend to. Egypt, for instance, had briefly withdrawn from Asia while concentrating, successfully, on fostering development and discipline at home. Rome, on the other hand, made large if transitory conquests to the east. Western civilization began a massive if ill-considered terraforming project on Mars, briefly succeeding in turning large sections of the northern hemisphere into a shallow sea. Everywhere there is ambition and success, but ambition within limits. Civilization knows the kind of thing it can do and what is beyond its reach. It busies itself, usually, with the former.

Despite this largely happy picture, the vitality of imperial society operates only at certain levels. Public enterprise in this epoch tends to take the form of gigantic canals, huge buildings and triumphal arches. The free enterprise section of the economy is able to grow only in the shadow of great, capital intensive initiatives, like the worldwide railroad building craze of the later nineteenth century. The enterprises which flourish in this period, however, are hardly models of entrepreneurial daring. They are, rather, often in the nature of utilities, made possible by the grant of official monopolies, of public land and licenses. Still, they are built in part with private money, and so have a modicum of private control in which the central government can as yet see no danger.

Cities, fussed over by paternalistic public authorities and businessmen anxious to stay in their good graces, approach a state of perfection. Transportation becomes as fast and safe as it will ever get, sanitary and health services proliferate to the extent of available knowledge. The police are everywhere effective through efficiency rather than brutality. Much of the economic activity of the period, both private and state-supported, is directed toward making public spaces beautiful and providing mass public entertainment. The latter was particularly the case in Western civilization, where the availability of electronic and neurally-induced illusion created an insatiable hunger for unmeditated experience.

The difference between this and previous ages of economic expansion, however, is that little of this activity really affects the way most people live. This is not an age of great increases in private consumption, or of new goods and services available to the typical household. Technological innovation as it applies to everyday life, in fact, comes to a halt, the first of many areas of mechanical ingenuity to follow. It is as if the wonders which civilizations produce during this period, the tunnels under the seas and the amphitheaters and great buildings, were happening on a level of reality different from that of ordinary life. The continuous change and excitement which were regarded as normal during the modern era continue, in a somewhat stereotyped fashion, on the public surface of the life of this period. Down below, where natural mankind lives, the stasis of everyday life which is native to the species already begins to return.

This is an age of perfect rather than daring art. The goal of the serious plastic and visual arts everywhere is the codification and mastery of historical styles. Syncretism and experiment are always possible, but command no durable respect. In an age of congealing standards, this is the time in which artists of all descriptions try to get it right, rather than to challenge or offend their audiences. Their audiences have access to the results of every possible experiment. It is no longer possible to challenge them.

Literature achieves final definition. For every imperial language (and some civilizations have more than one), the results of all the experiments of prior ages are long since in. It is only now, perhaps, that each language can become precisely itself, to do what only it can do and, for once, to do it without flaw. From the muscular, gnomic Latin of Tacitus' Annals to the sprung-rhyme lucidity of Those Who Err, greatest of English-language novels, the products of this period achieve a level of integrity which few in the time to come ever succeed in imitating.

This is the age when science dies. Even though the great final conclusions about the physical universe characteristic of each civilization had been reached two or three generations ago, this is the period in which they achieve their classical expression, the form in which they will be remembered forever after. Scientists, or natural philosophers, come to think of themselves in a way different from that of their predecessors. Their new role is not to discover new truths, or even necessarily to gather new information, but to teach and to apply the intellectual skills bequeathed by the past. Far from being rigid, however, they work always with an eye to synthesis. Because science is finished, they are more willing to consider those aspects of experience which cannot be captured by it. Their accounts of the world come more and more to resemble ontologies, theories of the whole of being which cover art and ethics and the supernatural.

This development is not simply a declination from old standards of rigor. Indeed, in a way it is a time of uniquely rigorous empiricism. What cannot be explained or reduced to something familiar is no longer simply explained away, as was the custom in prior ages. Rather, it is assigned a place in a hierarchy of knowledge. Even when some matter is held to be unknowable, it is still assigned a place on the new map of universal philosophy.

These maps, no matter which civilization composes them, call to a certain kind of fine mind in every other civilization which knows about them. The later Stoics and some types of Confucianism are examples, as are the mysticisms of Egypt and Islam, which became increasingly portable in this period. Schools and the writers of curricula love these systems. They are luminously clear, meticulously thorough, and beautifully expressed. They are also extremely artificial. The only comfort they offer is that of codifying a world in which there are no surprises. Like irony and the sort of sensibility which loves decay, they depend for their plausibility on the bland good fortune of their adherents. They fit ill with the experience of people whose life involves a great deal of wonder or misery, and many people's lives involve both. In later phases of civilization, the proportion of such people will increase.

Section Four: The Long Summer Afternoon (2244-2309)

"Although men be terrified by the signs appearing about the judgment day, yet before those signs begin to appear the wicked will think themselves to be in peace and security after the death of Antichrist and before the coming of Christ, seeing that the world is not at once destroyed as they thought hitherto."

--St. Thomas Aquinas
Summa Theologica

Readout

2246 A.D.
Islam, 1620. A.D.: The Turks defeat the Polish army at Jassy.
2247 A.D.
Egypt, 1300 B.C.: Officially, the period is called a Renaissance, a return to old patterns. The Renaissance is enforced by draconian police measures new in Egyptian history.
Egypt, 1300 B.C.: Magical and supernatural sanctions are invoked to assist the rule of law.
2257 A.D.
Egypt, 1290 B.C.: Ramses II comes to power, under whom the empire reaches its greatest extent.
2262 A.D.
Egypt, 1285 B.C.: Ramses II manages to avoid being killed at the Battle of Kadesh. Peace is made with Egypt's Asiatic enemies, the Hittites.
2264 A.D.:
China, 36 B.C.: Ch'en T'ang, a minor official, inflicts a stunning defeat on the Central Asian barbarians. The government considers punishing him for adventurism.

2265 A.D.

Rome, 138 A.D.: Antonius Pius becomes emperor, beginning the happiest era in civilized history.

2275 A.D.

Islam, 1649 A.D. Mohammed IV becomes Sultan after assassinating his father, Sultan Ibrahim.

2288 A.D.

Rome, 161 A.D.: General peace and prosperity prevail during most of the reign of the Stoic philosopher and emperor, Marcus Aurelius.

2289 A.D.

Islam, 1663 A.D.: The Turks invade the Holy Roman Empire.

2294 A.D.

Rome, 167 A.D.: Persistent border wars begin in the Balkans, taking up much of the Emperor's time.

2299 A.D.

Jan Sobieski defeats the Turks at Khorzim.

Rome, 180 A.D.: The demented emperor Commodus succeeds his father, Marcus Aurelius. Plague, famine and barbarian incursions break out. Commodus is assassinated after 12 years.

2309 A.D.

Islam: The Turks lay siege to Vienna; their army is routed.

China A.D.

The Former Han Dynasty is overthrown in a court intrigue by the dowager empress's nephew, Wang Mang, who becomes emperor.

Commentary

One of the recurring features of history, as indeed of everyday life, is the disclosure that one or another institution which was thought to be immeasurably strong had in fact become an empty shell. The least call on its resources or flexibility, and it collapses like a tree whose core has long-since rotted away, but which put forth leaves to the last. At some point during the seventy-odd years of this period, the empire of the world begins to die. Throughout the period, it appears stronger than ever, indeed wiser and more humane that it ever had before. Then, at the very end of the age, some little mishap occurs, some project is undertaken which strains the resources of the imperial government, and generations of order collapse into chaos overnight. The prestige that is lost among the barbarians is never wholly regained. Neither is the morale of civilized society at home.

The two generations before these catastrophes, however, are often considered the happiest in history. As a rule, the imperial government has the leisure to concern itself with both order and justice. The law tends to become rigid, but in large part because it is no longer problematical. Again, it is a question of ancient questions being answered and the results being reduced to final form. As a rule, the empire is not in an expansionist state of mind during this period. Those that are, like Egypt, soon realize that further adventures do not pay and settle down for a long period of peace. Where external barbarians make a nuisance of themselves, they are dealt with using the minimum of force necessary to maintain imperial prestige. Wisdom in this period consists in doing only what you have to do.

This attitude is possible because society lacks the energy to generate serious disorder. Further, it is necessary because the resources available to the imperial government have begun to decline. This stage of a civilization's life is one of small ambitions, of people who look no higher than to conventional success in established social and administrative hierarchies. This is not a period for empire builders, or even for reformist enthusiasts. Whatever ethnic or income group conflicts may exist in society have become so muted that internal police actions rarely require more than a show of force. Perhaps more important, the imagination necessary to plot revolt, or even to launch significant new economic ventures, is not encouraged by imperial culture. Actually, all civilizations do provide some outlet for people with the frontier spirit, since there are always border lands to be settled. This process, however, has no repercussions on human culture as a whole; it simply keeps the people involved from becoming disruptive. In the nature of things, it is always the border areas of civilization which collapse first when conspicuous decline sets in.

For the first time in the lives of some civilizations, the population of the world goes into a secular decline. Precisely why certain civilizations, such as Rome and China, began to experience prolonged population declines at about this time has long been a matter of debate. Even in civilizations where no manifest declines occur, still the empire never does better than stay stable, often soon being out-populated by barbarian neighbors. Doubtless, as was the case in the West, where better data are available, the declines had in fact begun in certain areas as long ago as the modern era. The usual reasons given are that the very expanse of civilization left it exposed to new diseases from beyond the borders, or that landholding patterns were such as to discourage the breaking up of family plots among many children. All these explanations are inadequate.

The fact of the matter is, the human world begins to shrink in intensity, if not necessarily yet in space. Large, new projects in any sphere of life become rare. Capital expenditures for plant tend more and more to be tied up in the maintenance of old facilities, rather than in the creation of new ones. Indeed, major existing facilities, from viaducts to airports, become proportionately ever more costly to repair as the number of people served by them first levels off and then declines.

The kind of economic decline which occurs in this period is quite different from that represented by the normal business cycle (which in fact continues). Markets and labor slowly disappear. Capital becomes proportionately more abundant for lack of productive enterprises in which to invest it, so much so that the economic life of the period is troubled by an irrational rise in the value of land and tangible assets. The activities of the imperial government, far from absorbing capital needed elsewhere, have instead the effect of masking what would otherwise have been a series of ever-deeper economic slumps.

Indeed, activities at all levels of public life sometimes give the impression of being conducted merely for lack of anything else to keep the participants occupied. Important local citizens and civic associations continue to perform good works and found cultural institutions that duplicate existing facilities and sometimes merely annoy the beneficiaries. Serious culture comes more and more to resemble ritual, even if it has no religious content. Old plays are performed and books are read primarily because they provide a common frame of reference for persons of refined taste. The respect for the canon becomes superstitious. Criticism of these works becomes both more formal and wildly inaccurate, as the learned lose the ability to see what the classics meant when they were new. The tendency grows to look for magical and prophetic qualities in the texts.

There have been many periods in history when societies in comfortable circumstances realized that their happy state was not maintainable, that in fact they stood at the edge of an abyss. For some reason, such sentiments were rare in this period, even in civilizations such as China and the West which were always prone to attacks of apocalyptic anxiety. It is as if the cultural reflexes needed to foresee and deal with impending danger, even in imagination, had atrophied in the long years since world unification. It is, therefore, not a complete surprise that a fairly trivial event, something that in former ages could have been dealt with without much trouble, in this period is yet sufficient to show just how little resilience the structure of civilization retained.

The surest sign of weakness in any society is a dependence on good rulers. In this period, all civilizations but Egypt acquired unsatisfactory ones and promptly paid the price. The successor to Marcus Aurelius, his son Commodus, succeeded to power in a perfectly regular fashion. Though grossly unsuited for the job, his administration would not have brought ruin to the empire were it not for the fact that none of the ruling strata had the initiative to deal with the multiple (but perfectly manageable) problems with which the empire was faced. His assassination, though perhaps necessary, was not evidence of political imagination. In China, the usurper Wang Mang became emperor through an irregular court intrigue, but Han constitutional punctilio was not so outraged as to necessitate the downfall of the imperial regime. It was his gimcrack "reformist" ideas, which in this age of respect for authority no one could oppose until too late, which did that. In the West, the conversion of the unstable Emperor Friedrich to the New Eugenics faction at court, with the subsequent worldwide revulsion at the methods of the new ministry, simply showed that a government of technocrats is no more resistant to the intrigues of ambitious cranks than is one of soldiers or priests. In Islam, perhaps the saddest case of all, an earnest Sultan decided to renew the jihad against the West in such a way as to establish the supremacy of the Ottoman Empire in western Eurasia once and for all. The attempt was a hundred years too late, and the defeat demoralized the Empire to such an extent that it never really recovered.

Third Transition: The World Begins to Crack
(2309-2322)

"How very amusing! Actually attacking our camp! Most amusing."

--Remark of a responsible British officer on the occasion of the Isandlwana massacre in Zululand (1879)

Readout

2310 A.D.
China, 10 A.D.: Emperor Wang Mang attempts to create a reactionary utopia based on a literal reading of the Confucian classics.
2311 A.D.
China, 11 A.D.: The texts of the classics are doctored to support the usurper's position.
2313 A.D.
Islam, 1687 A.D.: The Turks are defeated at Mohacs in Hungary; Sultan Mohammed IV is deposed and succeeded by Suleiman III.
2320 A.D.
Rome, 193 A.D.: Order is restored by the soldier emperor Septimus Severus, who eventually dies while trying to repair the defenses of Britain.
2322 A.D.
China, 22 A.D.: Wang Mang is overthrown. Civil war and peasant revolt follow.

Commentary

The disasters of this period are almost exclusively of internal origin, though we see the beginning of the fraying of the empire at the edges and its gradual loss of control over its strategic environment. The cause which each of these crises has in common is an irresponsible nostalgia on the part of the ruling circles for a somewhat imaginary past. The best example of this is the Chinese emperor, Wang Mang. Historians have never regarded him as a "real" emperor, but simply as a usurper, despite the fact he had more influence on Chinese history than all but a handful of rulers. It was his intent to create the communal and non-hierarchical society which has been the fantasy of one wing of Chinese social thought throughout its history. It would be a world without private property or any but the most minimal government apparatus.

It was the belief of this ideologue and his deluded adherents that the utopia of his imagination had actually existed in the first phase of the Chou Dynasty, long before the Era of Contending States. The Confucian system of statecraft, from this point of view, was originally intended to define just such a utopia. Wang Mang produced versions of some of the Confucian classics which supposedly dated from before the great bookburning by the First Emperor. This version of the classics became known as the "Old Texts," as distinguished from the "New Texts" reconstructed by scholars from memory during the early period of imperial history. The fraud was not completely exposed for another 1,500 years.

The Old Texts lacked much of the ethical and teleological content which may have been present in original Confucianism and which in any event had been characteristic features of social and political discourse during the Han period. The effect of these features had been to add flexibility and humanity to government practice. The Old Text school idealized an unreachable past and held out no particular hope for the future. Though much more "this worldly" than other forms of Confucianism before and since, the Old Texts do not appear to have facilitated rational decision-making in the next phase of Chinese history. As for

Wang Mang, his attempt to create an anarchist utopia through the use of imperial power had predictable results. His body was found by insurgent forces in the great hall of his deserted palace. He died by his own hand in ceremonial costume, his ideological supporters having long-since absented themselves.

In Islam, the final failure to destroy the Holy Roman Empire reflected a more purely military incapacity, but the lesson was all the more striking for a regime which defined success in almost purely military terms. Mohammed IV, like Wang Mang, was a romantic. His society, as he understood it, was justified by the duty to carry out the jihad, an enterprise which had long since been defined as the conversion to Islam by the West. What made him unusual, and fatal, was his decision to make this largely metaphysical goal a matter of immediate policy. He saw no reason why his empire could not return to the project initiated by the first Caliphs of the seventh and eighth centuries. The fact that Europe was no longer inhabited by semibarbarian hordes, or that his own people lacked the enthusiasm or technique to sustain such an offensive, was not relevant to his calculations. The empire won many wars after the catastrophe before Vienna, but it never really left the defensive again.

The Empire of the West in the twenty-fourth century, for its part, attempted by a sheer act of imperial will to return to the glory days of the Age of Discovery, to break new ground as in the miraculous decades from Columbus to Galileo. It became policy to create a New Man within human society and a far vaster colonial empire beyond the limits of Earth. The New Eugenics "party," as the bureaucratic clique anachronistically styled itself, supported both these initiatives.

Ironically, the immediate causes of their fall from public favor were the small scale reforms with which they concerned themselves. Not the least repugnant of these was a concerted effort at "standardization" of the ornament in public places throughout the world, inspired by the somewhat garish Baroque revival then popular among designers and art historians.

The actual eugenics project itself did succeed in creating a strain of large, highly intelligent, but singularly incurious post-human hominids. Called "The New People," some thousands of juveniles had been produced by the time the government fell. They were then simply put up for adoption like human children and left largely unregarded by later administrations, with the expectation that they would simply disappear into the world population. This policy was a mistake. The New People were not interfertile with human beings and never identified with human society. In fact, they manifested a disconcerting penchant for anthropophagy during times of social disorder, when consumer goods became rare and police supervision non-existent. In later years they posed a considerable police problem, finally becoming the last and most terrifying of history's "barbarians."

The palace mutiny and assassination of the emperor, however, were occasioned by a far more prosaic event, the refusal of the Special Forces to send one more draft of conscript emigrants to the colonies against their will. The Europa settlement was quarantined because of yet another infestation of "pseudo-biologicals" during this period as far as returns to Earth were concerned, but coercive immigration was actually increased. (Though the emigration to Europa was finally halted, the quarantine was never lifted, even after the colony had clearly ceased to exist.) The largest single failure in terms of expense was on Mars. There, the sullen and overcrowded inhabitants of the hopefully named "afforestation villages" watched in dismay as the terraforming process created a methane-tainted atmosphere which was not only unbreathable but (locally) actually explosive. The single most serious cause of resentment against the government, however, was created by the attempt to "reintegrate" the government with civil society through the (literal) regimentation of the latter, particularly as this program applied to the emperor's policy of compulsory parenthood.

Even after basic discipline in the military was restored, the loss of prestige to the imperial government, which after all justified itself largely in terms of management skills and technical expertise, was never wholly made good.

As for the Roman Emperor Commodus, he believed that he could be as irresponsible as Alexander the Great. He ruled an empire that was just capable, with great care and a certain amount of luck, in maintaining its borders and providing some basic services to at least the inhabitants of the major cities. His decision to turn away from the hardworking prudence of his father was, in a sense, a return to the "Classical" spirit. Concern for the far away, for the distant in time, even for the purely theoretical, never fit that well into the political life of this civilization. Though of course every great society must do some long-range thinking, Classical societies had always put this off as long as possible. What else could be the case in a civilization which, in its youth, had favored limiting the terms of key offices to a year and selecting the incumbents by lot? After decades of cautious good government, the emperor's successor (by right of birth and not of adoption by his predecessor, as most of the best emperors had been, including Augustus), Commodus sought to rule by improvisation, to seek popular acclaim, to let the dead bury their dead. Though Commodus himself may never have drawn the parallel, his behavior was comparable to Alexander's, who from sheer high spirits conquered all the world he knew about (indeed, more than all) with nothing but ingenuity and good luck. The difference, of course, was that Alexander came from a growing civilization. In any event, his base of support was so small he had very little to lose. Commodus, and the strange parade of imperial pretenders who immediately succeeded him, had the world to lose, and no one was making any more of it.

Assassinations were not unknown in the life of any civilization before this period. Neither, for that matter, was the occasional military revolt. What is surprising during this Transition is the degree and length of disorder which attended these otherwise commonplace events, at least in some civilizations. Some of the ephemeral emperors during the crisis were elected or otherwise chosen through constitutional processes, some were chosen by the soldiers, and some chose themselves. Almost all, however, had a short lifespan and never succeeded in gaining control outside their capitals. Indeed, for the first time since modernity, we get here a hint of a world which is no longer effectively under the control of one master.

Part III: Decline and Fall (2322-2520)

Far-called, our navies melt away;
On dune and headland sinks the fire:
Lo, all our pomp of yesterday
Is one with Nineveh and Tyre!

--Rudyard Kipling
  Recessional

At the beginning of this period of roughly two centuries, the world is much as it has been since late modernity. It is near the peak of population, and the economy which supports it operates ecumenically. Society as a whole is generally prosperous. Though culture in all its forms has become increasingly formalized, a high level of technique is everywhere available and everywhere practiced. The world is essentially a single political unit, ruled by an absolute but distant monarchy, which in theory rules with pragmatic benevolence. Life for most people, most of the time, is predictable and generally tolerable.

At the end of the period, this world is literally in ruins. Except where neighboring or succeeding civilizations have extended their influence, urban life is in retreat. The arts and sciences of civilization are increasingly unavailable outside a dwindling number of ancient centers of culture. Much of the world, in fact, has collapsed into thinly populated barbarism. The imperial government is almost everywhere acknowledged as the only legitimate universal authority, and just as widely ignored. The central government can provide neither police nor military security. Different regions rule themselves, or go ungoverned. The apparatus of the state has largely disappeared beyond the capital and a few strongholds. The imperial office itself, while no longer routinely transferred by assassination and coup, is becoming increasingly ceremonial. Such affairs as the central government can still concern itself with have a ritualistic, even metaphysical cast.

This is the time after the Future, a period when most civilizations begin to seem more and more alike in their decay. Certainly they suffer from uncannily similar misfortunes. Every characteristic task which a civilization might have hoped to achieve was accomplished in previous epochs. In this period, every great civilized society, no matter its pretensions or its hopes, its goodwill or its actual accomplishments, must "join the majority." No matter the level of technology theoretically available, there has always been an appalling consistency to the lives of ordinary people in every settled society. This study of the fate of civilizations is about nothing more than an interruption in this common level of human existence, the passing season of fantasy and hubris which constitute civilization.

None of this lasts. Nothing has changed. The universe is holographic; every point of space subsumes every other point. Past, present and future are always accessible. Heaven and Hell are coincident. How could anything ever be different?

The people of this period, particularly the educated, developed concerns alien to those of their predecessors of even two generations before. Spengler called this the "Second Religiousness," the return of serious interest in the basic questions of existence, accompanied often by an appalling gullibility for religious charlatans and manufactured miracles. As we noted, the first stirrings of this phase of spiritual life began as early as the First Transition, and may even be traced back to latest modernity. However, the glory of the Empire tended to drown out the still, small voice. With the glory faded, the voice becomes more insistent.

This is the period when Buddhism was accepted in China, when Christianity, against the odds, supplanted the ancient ideology of the Roman state, when the cheerful land of Egypt became the grim kingdom of priestly hierarchy and dark wisdom known to later times. Even Islam, transfixed though it was by the fireworks of Western technological supremacy, began to cultivate an adamantine fundamentalism which came to fruition after the end of the universal state.

One historian has called this development the "victory of barbarism and religion," while another referred to it as "the loss of nerve." Other historians have seen in it an awakening by troubled civilized societies to what really matters in life. Because government is unreliable and the arts are increasingly corrupt, because every worldly hope has been seen to fail, people have the opportunity to look beyond the world of the senses, to seek again for the entrance to eternity. Certainly the change in the preoccupations of the thinking classes cannot be put down simply to laziness and fear. The mood began to change at the top, among the best spirits, before it spread to a wider public and produced the carnival of magic and wonderworkers which attends the final stage of every civilization. The intellectual systems created during this period, in fact, are among the most interesting and internally consistent artifacts of the human mind. Neoplatonism and Taoism, fantasticated versions of classical philosophies, should be on the agenda for any student who wishes to understand the full range of philosophic thought.

Still, it is not these highly refined systems which necessarily come to dominate a civilization's life, but a revelation of some sort, a personal link to the numinous which the great philosophies can hope to support but never to prove. The victory of these originally demotic religions is made possible by the new predisposition of the cultured elites to give them a hearing. What sounds like a joke becomes fact in those days: skepticism becomes skeptical even of itself, so that the best educated can again view the world with the uncorrupted innocence of the dawn of their civilization. The triumph of Christianity is the great example of this process, but the half-digested Buddhism of the Latter Han Dynasty is certainly at least analogous. In those societies, where indigenous religion had usually been the complacent servant of the state, the adoption of alien cults was to some extent an expression of popular disgust with the imperial regime. In Egypt and the West, in which priestly hierarchies had traditionally stood alongside of, and to some extent in opposition to, the rulers of this world, the Second Religiousness was in the nature of a great revival, a return to traditional forms of piety. In the ultimate West, indeed, the pope came again to have a veto over the appointment of a nominee to the imperial dignity.

In military and other secular matters, the period of decay is characterized by reliance on personal command and centralization in all fields of life, coupled with a simultaneous collapse of discipline in all spheres in which this strategy is attempted. Why this loss of skill in operating large organizations should occur, and in so many contexts, is not self-evident. Some might argue that modernity and the Future tend to shake men lose from traditional family and other communal ties, leaving them irresponsible enough to try their luck wherever ambition makes success plausible. If this were the case, however, how could it be that the world was growing more peaceful for most of the time since the end of modernity? As for family ties, the politics of this period is relentlessly dynastic, even in civilizations where governments have not normally been organized on the dynastic principle. On the other hand, it may be that the more contemplative nature of the intellectual life of late civilizations has the effect of making people more likely to consult their own conscience than either tradition or authority, and they find that their conscience is a light taskmaster. Whatever the cause, we see everywhere the paradox of the rulers of the age of decline coming to practice a politics no less primitive than that of their barbarian adversaries.

The upshot is that, for much of this age of decay, the forces of the imperium rarely serve the central authority with any degree of reliability. Every successful commander is a potential usurper. The ambitions of these men are often restrained by nothing more than the sad fact that the forces they lead are quite as unreliable as their commanders. As the security forces of the central authority become more and more the instruments of civil war, they necessarily also become less and less effective against external threats. In some cases, they decay into little more than a guard for the capital. Curiously, colonies founded on largely unoccupied territory show a far greater tendency to try to break away from the empire than do ancient civilizations which had long been simply occupied by imperial forces. The latter become little more than prizes for would-be Caesars.

Section One: The Search for Order (2322-2376)

"You know the rent is in arrears;
the dog has not been fed in years;
it's even worse than it appears;
but it's all right."

--The Grateful Dead
  Touch of Gray

Readout

2323 A.D.
Egypt, 1224 B.C.: Ramses II dies after 76 years of vainglory and building shoddy monuments to his own importance.
2327 A.D.
Rome, 200 A.D.: Neoplatonism comes to dominate the thinking of the educated.
2334 A.D.
Rome, 217 A.D.: Vicious Emperor Caracalla dies.
2336 A.D.
China, 36 A.D.: The Latter (or Eastern) Han Dynasty is established. The capital and centers of power move east.
2337 A.D.
China, 37 A.D.: The empire adopts a laissez faire economic policy and a defensive military posture.
2340 A.D.
Islam, 1714 A.D.: Tripoli becomes effectively independent of the empire.
2345 A.D.
Rome, 218 A.D.: Heliogabalus misrules the empire, or at least the City of Rome, for four years.
Egypt, 1202 B.C.: A brief interregnum occurs, during part of which the land is ruled by a Syrian adventurer.

2347 A.D..
Rome, 220 A.D.: Goths invade Asia Minor and the Balkan
Peninsula.
2349 A.D.
Rome, 222 A.D.: Alexander Severus, another soldier emperor
and perhaps a crypto-Christian, hold the empire together.
2350 A.D.
Egypt, 1197 B.C.: Set-nakt establishes the Twentieth Dynasty.
2357 A.D.
Egypt, 1190 B.C.: Ramses III defends his northeastern border
against the Sea Peoples.
2358 A.D.
China, 58 A.D.: The Emperor Ming-Ti introduces Buddhism.
2360 A.D.
China, 60 A.D.: The historian Pan Ku writes the definitive history
of the Former Han Dynasty.
2362 A.D.
Rome, 235 A.D.: Severus is murdered and six emperors succeed
in six years.
2364 A.D.
Islam, 1738 A.D.: The Turks defeat an Austro-Russian alliance.
2371 A.D.
Rome, 244 A.D.: Emperor Philip the Arabian reigns briefly.
2376 A.D.
Rome, 249 A.D.: The harsh but efficient Emperor Decius
maintains order and institutes a vigorous persecution of
Christians.

Commentary

There is a certain relief in reaching this point in the tale of a
civilization's life. The prior age was like a period in the life of an
old family which became more proper and socially exacting as
its underlying fortune declined. Finally, when bankruptcy comes
and the old estate has to be sold, the crisis can be acknowledged.
No one cares if you don't dress for dinner or if you leave a car on

blocks in the yard. There is no need to keep up appearances, since there are far more interesting things to worry about.

Throughout the period of decline, civilization is prone to external attacks of various kinds which it is only barely competent to deal with. It is an old saw that an empire organizes its enemies to defeat it; the very existence of concentrated wealth and a non-combatant population attracts marginal peoples to the borders with an eye to trade and occasional plunder. These peoples have sometimes been called the "external proletariat." With time, they acquire many of the skills of civilized societies, creating a pale of loosely-organized barbarian states radiating from the civilized core areas. While in its heyday the empire can keep this gray region more or less policed, in its decline this is no longer possible. The barbarians often see that some region of the empire is undefended because the central government's attention is focused on internal affairs.

Sometimes, these invaders are barely more than savages off the steppe, attracted by legends of the wealth of the settled lands. Sometimes, they are civilized societies in their own right with long-term strategic goals. This was the situation Islam faced. It is possible for the difference between an "external" and an "internal" proletariat to be largely theoretical, particularly when the empire contains large chunks of primitive alien societies which never became "developed" in the way that the core areas did. It is the regions of immemorial banditry, such as Central Asia and Anatolia, the Balkans and the American Southwest, which easily become regions where the emperor's writ does not run, and the only "public services" are reprisal raids from the central government.

This pattern is to be distinguished from the behavior of old and populous cultures caught in another civilization's empire. As we noted above, these are scarcely much of a threat to the empire's real integrity. They can and do produce inchoate revolts and even real nationalist insurrections. Always, however, these are the work either of peasant enthusiasts or of romantic urban intellectuals. So ingrained does the habit of civilization become in regions like Egypt and India, China and Western Europe, that they soon reach accommodation with whoever seems most likely to promote order in the long term. Nationalism is a disease of modernity, and even the chauvinism which marks all mature civilizations tends to fade out as both dominator and dominated reach comparable levels of decrepitude.

The unambiguously internal proletariat creates problems in only some civilizations during this period. When it does, the result is simply the pointless vandalism of people who think themselves ill-used, but who literally cannot imagine a state of things fundamentally different from the present order. Revolts are in the nature of an appeal to the central government for the redress of grievances, usually involving corrupt or incompetent local authorities. The real sources of disorder during this epoch are the ruling class itself. The outrages committed by the imperial government during the Third Transition robbed it of much of its sacred character. The temporary collapse of the administration also proved to all the limits of its power. It now seems, to the local police and army commanders, to lesser members of the imperial family, even to merely opulent citizens, that just anyone can aspire to the highest office. The result is, often enough, "just anybody" does in fact achieve it. Indeed, this is the last era in which there can be really eccentric world rulers. None of them last long, but their antics are a delight for moralists to condemn in all later ages.

A more interesting feature of the political history of the period, however, is the degree of good government it somehow manages to provide, even against the odds. In Roman history, during a long slice of this epoch, the empire came close to being governed in the way its "constitution" prescribed, with the emperor elected by and responsible to the Senate. In other civilizations, there was at least a period of successful rally against incipient chaos, of partial reforms and much selfless devotion to duty. The very bursting of the illusion that the world had entered a permanent golden age, that Ramses II would be Pharaoh forever or that the Roman peace was magically unbreakable, inspired a degree of initiative and original thinking which had not been seen since the beginning of the imperial era. Of course, the thinking was along the lines of "How can we stop this fatal trend from getting out of hand?", but still it constituted an improvement over the simple search for precedent and scurrying to save face which passed for statecraft in more comfortable phases of the empire's life.

At ground level, we have the first whiff during this period, not just of economic decline, but of the physical collapse of civilized life. Ancient infrastructures, from aqueducts to communication satellites, are ill-repaired or not repaired at all. While the government begins, and sometimes even finishes, large prestige projects, the machinery of everyday life becomes less reliable. Amenities begin to be too expensive for the lower classes, and in some cases wholly unobtainable. Particularly, communications and travel become more difficult and sporadically dangerous. Though the population is stable or in decline, basic subsistence begins to come into question. Food production and transport lose the clockwork efficiency which some universal states achieved in their younger days. Prior stages of the imperial era might have been troubled by "food crises," when prices rose beyond the means of ordinary citizens. As the decline deepens, what in the past would have been mere distribution bottlenecks threaten to become true famines.

While this world is showing ever greater signs of wear and tear, both the heights of society and its depths are increasingly concerned with the other world. At the top, the last generation of "intellectuals," as that class had existed (under various names) since the days of modernity, is putting the finishing touches on systems of thought which link the natural, human and divine in a single apprehension of reality. Down below, the immemorial religion of mankind, of amulets and holy men and holy places, is reviving in new forms. Whatever hold the skepticisms of high culture had ever had on popular culture swiftly melt away as the traditional objections to the spiritual life cease to persuade even the educated.

More ominous, however, is the antinomian streak which sometimes infects both the ancient and the novel devotions that grow in popularity with the triumph of the Second Religiousness. Sometimes, these new faiths are shot through with vivid images of revenge and strange ambitions for the faithful, with hatred against the order of things and half-furtive notions of a future whose shape freezes the blood of such of the uninitiated who hear of it.

These demotic cults tend to rise up the social scale more than even the popularized versions of the systems of the educated tend to fall. Though the cults may be phrased in the language of philosophy when they come to be expounded by philosophers, their power at all levels of society is visceral, numinous, unanswerable.

The last intellectuals inhabit this period for the same reason that the last true scientists died out more than a century before: what they had to do was just about finished. The term intellectual has been variously defined. Perhaps it is most aptly used with regard to people who make their living by devising new systems of thought. Artists may or may not fit into this category; it depends on the degree to which they are conscious of the systemic implications of their creations. The systems produced in this period, when "all the data are in," when people at least believe that have a complete account of the natural world, when everything bad and good that can happen in history has already happened, when all arts are finished, these systems are really and truly final.

Everything has been accounted for. The supposedly final philosophical systems developed at the beginning of Winter, the philosophies of the Aristotelians and the Confucians, were as much concerned with denying or denigrating areas of experience or belief as they were with trying to be comprehensive; they "explained" only a congenial residue of life. This is not the case with the truly final systems like Neoplatonism or late Taoism or Mahayana Buddhism, which really do explain everything from pond scum to the Mind of God. Having settled these matters, there is really very little left to say.

After this epoch, there is still a class of teachers and researchers, there are still large and well-attended institutions of higher learning, there is even some of the most poignant and skilful historical and memoirist writing ever composed. All of this, however, has ceased to live. In future ages, people will die to preserve the treasures of the civilization, because they know themselves incapable of creating any more.

Section Two: The Duty to Work (2376-2447)

"If we would set against the Roman "panem et circenses" [bread and circuses] (the final life-symbol of Epicurean-Stoic existence, and, at bottom, of Indian existence also) some corresponding symbol of the North (and of Old China and Egypt) it would be the 'Right to Work.' This was the basis of Fichte's thoroughly Prussian (and now European) conception of State-Socialism, and in the last terrible stages of evolution it will culminate in the Duty to Work."

--Oswald Spengler
  The Decline of the West

Readout

2377 A.D.
Egypt, 1170 B.C.: Workers on state enterprises increasingly go unpaid. Unpaid foreign mercenaries begin to afflict the countryside.
2383 A.D.
Egypt, 1164 B.C.: Ramses III killed in a harem conspiracy
2384 A.D.
Rome, 257 A.D.: Visigoths and Ostrogoths invade the Black Sea area.
Rome, 257 A.D.: Franks invade Spain, Alemanni and Suevi invade Upper Italy.
2387 A.D.
Egypt, 1160 B.C.: Egypt gradually withdraws from Asia, finally leaving the Palestinian mines unworked.
Egypt, 1160 B.C.: A long period of serious inflation sets in.
2390 A.D.
Egypt, 1157 B.C.: The Empire comes to an end for Egypt. The government is thereafter concerned wholly with defense of the homeland.

2394 A.D.

Egypt, 1153 B.C.: The Pharaoh is depicted on the same scale as the priestly oligarchy. The office loses executive power.

2395 A.D.

Rome, 268 A.D.: Goths sack Athens.

2397 A.D.

Rome, 270 A.D.: The Emperor Aurelian restores the borders and suppresses rebellion.

2410 A.D.

Islam, 1784 A.D.: The Crimea is ceded to Russia.

2411 A.D.

Rome, 284 A.D.: Diocletian carries out a thorough civil and military reform of the empire. Vigorous persecution of Christians by this superstitious man.

2415 A.D.

Islam, 1789: The Austrians take Belgrade.

2416 A.D.

Islam, 1790 A.D.: The Sultan attempts systematic westernizing reforms. This theme dominates the rest of the Empire's history.

2424 A.D.

Islam, 1798 A.D.: Napoleon conquers Egypt but abandons it soon after.

2431 A.D.

Islam, 1805 A.D.: Mehemet Ali makes Egypt effectively independent of the Empire. He transforms the economy with a vast system of forced labor and state enterprise.

2433 A.D.

Islam, 1807 A.D.: Sultan Selim III is deposed and succeeded by Mustafa.

Islam, 1807 A.D.: The Greeks declare independence; the Turks attempt to suppress the rebellion.

2442 A.D.

Egypt, 1105 B.C.: Major temples are sacked in popular uprisings and the southern army commander revolts.

2447 A.D.

Rome, 320 A.D.: Constantine the Great moves the capital to Constantinople and legalizes Christianity.

2447 A.D.
Egypt, 1100 B.C.: Revolt against the High Priest of Amon, Amen-hotep, who had long dominated the government.

Commentary

This age defines a lifetime in which the conservative authoritarians of the world finally come into their own. The necessity for a return to ancient discipline seems the foremost need of the time, and the world does not lack for disciplinarian taskmasters to provide it. This is not a time of overweening ambition, like the tyranny that ended modernity, nor an era in which the rulers of the world indulge their nostalgia for a romantic past, as was the case in the Third Transition. If this is an age of reactionaries, the "reaction" here is a matter of hard necessity, of ruthless enforcement of order and rigid standards, not to implement the self-expression of some great individual's will, but because there no longer exists the room for maneuver which is necessary if individual rights and local peculiarities are to be respected. Justice the imperial government can still provide, at least on occasion. Mercy is increasingly beyond its capacity.

The last phase of discipline comes in response to the calamitous external environment. In this period, Egypt loses its foreign empire entirely, first from indigenous revolt, and finally because of the rise of terrible new empires in Mesopotamia. Rome suffers an explosion of invasions by various barbarian peoples who spread havoc to regions of the empire that had known peace almost from the days of the Republic. In the Empire of the West, the Martian colonies, vastly overextended but chronically underfunded, are effectively abandoned by the terrestrial authorities to whatever fate they can negotiate with their increasingly bizarre environment. Meanwhile, military adventurers from Afghanistan and southern Africa began insurrections which brought them in sight of the twin North Atlantic capitals. In Islam, the empire in Europe loses ground to the Austrians and the Russians in a series of wars which seem destined to end in the loss of Istanbul itself.

Throughout the world, ordinary life is endangered by casual violence from the ungoverned powerful and ruthless bands of the desperate poor. Almost everywhere, normal arrangements for the production and distribution of goods cease to function. There is no more basis for long-term economic growth. Science has long since ceased to produce exploitable ideas. Within the limits of natural knowledge, engineering has exhausted the fund of possible innovations. Occasionally, new systems and skills can be developed for special purposes, but there is no more flow of world-renewing invention, even in the Empire of the West. The maximum possible extension of business enterprises, both in terms of geography and productivity, had long ago been reached. It is clear to all that the return from new endeavors is almost invariably negative. The life of mankind has again become a zero-sum game, where the increase of one person's slice of the pie reduces the slices of the rest. Further, the pie is shrinking.

The economies of all civilizations in this phase are "premodern," no matter the technological foundations on which they rest. They do not naturally expand, and nothing new, not even the repairs needed after war or natural disaster, is done unless someone in authority orders it. In China, where the government consciously tried to avoid the Legalist economic policy of the Former Han period, the orders were often not given. The laissez faire economic strategy of the Latter Han, with its Taoist faith in the ability of society to find its own proper level, was in its way as counterintuitive to Chinese rulers as centralized planning was to rulers of most other civilizations.

The pattern that characterizes this period, in fact, may simply be that it reverses the economic outlook which prevailed in the early empire. Thus, civilizations with the habit of free enterprise often abandon it in this phase of their history. Certainly in Rome, and even more in the West, there were men who were prepared to issue the necessary orders for the whole world, down to the last nut and bolt and brick

Diocletian reformed the administrative system of the empire from top to bottom. To a large extent, it was restructured along military lines: certainly it was intended to serve military purposes. His most famous reform was the division of the empire into four regions, each under the command of an emperor of greater or lesser seniority. This division ultimately split the empire into an eastern and a western half, the former becoming the cradle of Magian (or Islamic) civilization, the latter a hunting ground for barbarians. In this period, however, Diocletian's most pronounced effect on everyday life came from his attempt to control the economy, particularly the terrifying price increases at the retail level. Later historians have been appalled at the crudity with which this was done: the imperial edicts on price control do not trouble to distinguish between wholesale and retail. Workers and their descendants were fixed in their trades by law. The demand of the government for tax monies was insatiable, and the ferocity of the tax farmers who were subcontracted to collect these sums tended to drive such business as there was underground. It discouraged all enterprises which were not actually imperially licensed monopolies.

In the Empire of the later West, which had a subtle knowledge of the uses and limits of command economics and far greater ability to monitor economic activity generally, things were far, far worse. Money, in fact if not in law, was abolished and replaced by a cybernetic rationing system. Every conceivable occupation was either licensed or prohibited, and everyone was answerable to an imperial inspector. Even retirees were technically "low recall priority reserve workers," and still had to fill out time-use forms at the end of every week. This system did manage to keep staple foods and basic utilities available in most urban areas. For certain sections of the administrative classes and the emperor's corps of occultic "New Philosophers," it provided luxuries that were literally priceless. What it did not provide, despite the increasingly draconian penalties for failure to implement government directives, was the possibility of self-sustaining economic growth, or even an honest chance of maintaining the current system.

The imperial government did not simply recapitulate the errors of command-economy totalitarian states of the twentieth century; it developed far more advanced ones, made possible by the availability of information processing technology and a generally higher level of engineering expertise. The imperial government, for instance, tried to design cyclical fluctuations into the operation of the world economy when it became apparent that the secular trend was a slow, irregular slide. It even attempted to reproduce the beneficent effects of technological innovation by periodically introducing and then withdrawing a range of existing technologies. Despite the warnings of history, the empire tried to replace dying regional industrial networks with gigantic, vertically integrated, single-facility production units. These "terminal factories," each the size of a small mountain, were often placed in delicate, historically significant but long de-industrialized landscapes, such as central Honshu or the southern shore of Lake Michigan. They eventually became empty, ominous hulks, the objects of superstitious awe to later cultures, to which they represented the power and the downfall of the West.

For Islam, this was the beginning of the sad attempt by the Sultan's government to import just enough Western armament and mechanical expertise to give the empire's armies a fighting chance. The process was long delayed by the inability of the theoretically omnipotent autocrat to reform or abolish the Janissaries. This slave army, at one time recruited with the child-tax on Eastern European Christians, was so loyal to the Sultan and the empire as to seem to exempt him from the need to practice mere human politics when dealing with his subjects. In this epoch, their loyalty, and that of the mullahs who formed the other great pillar of the Sultanate, did not preclude the assassination of any imperial incumbent who seemed to be trying to tinker with their immemorial privileges. Thus, for some years, the reform process had to proceed piecemeal, with many reverses and half-hearted measures. The true analogue of Diocletian in the Islamic world of this epoch was the Sultan's nominal vassal, the Khedive Mehemet Ali of Egypt. He imported European industries wholesale and trained a respectable modern army with European advisers, paying for it all with the forced labor of the peasants of the Nile Delta and with slaves from the south.

Ancient Egypt was never quite the "hydraulic despotism" of sociological fantasy (that is, a society where the government maintains absolute control because of the need to build and repair an extensive irrigation system). On the other hand, it had always been a fairly dirigiste society. Large projects were almost invariably government sponsored. The economic decay of this period, therefore, was largely expressed by the government doing less well what it had always done before. The land became shabbier than it had been in former ages, workers went on strike when asked to work for nothing (which was all that their government supervisors had to give), the loyalty of the army became problematical. Clerical authority became more and more absolute as the priesthood of Amon came close to swallowing the civil government. Though this was an age of growing interest in magic and of the practice of piety at all levels of society, the hierarchy was not well-placed to benefit from the fact. Their favorite cult, that of Amon, the Hidden God, had never been popular, though in a way he had been the necessary lynchpin to the Egyptian pantheon. It was the accessible old gods, Isis and Osiris and Horus, in whom the people hoped. That the servants of the Hidden God should gain control of the state was a further cause of alienation of the rulers from the ruled.

Like the highly Neoplatonized "astral piety" which Diocletian hoped to make the universal religion as he strove to stamp out Christianity, the hegemony of Amon and his priests was a feature of a time of unsustainable reaction. The reaction here, of course, was not to some supposed force of universal progress, but simply to the natural process of dying. The collapse of the reaction also triggered a rejection of the reactionaries' theology. At the end of the era, the gods changed, or the old gods came back.

Section Three: The Sick Man (2447-2481)

"The Padishah Emperor has commanded me to take this fief and end all dispute."

--Frank Herbert
  Dune

Readout

2450 A.D.
Islam, 1824 A.D.: The Greeks defeat the Turks at Mitylene.
2453 A.D.
Islam, 1827 A.D.: The Turkish-Egyptian fleet is destroyed by a French-British-Russian task force at Navarino.
2456 A.D.
Islam, 1830 A.D.: The French take Algeria.
2457 A.D.
Egypt, 1090 B.C.: Rule of the country is divided between General Heri-Hor and the merchant princes of Tanis. Ramses XI dies in obscurity, taking the dynasty with him.
Egypt, 1090 B.C.: The Twenty-First Dynasty begins. The country remains disunited.
Islam, 1831 A.D.: Muslim Egyptians briefly hold Syria.
2462 A.D.
Egypt, 1085 B.C.: Egypt is divided into several small states. The power of Libya grows.
2464 A.D.
Rome, 337 A.D.: In accordance with Diocletian's reform, the empire is divided into east and west for administrative purposes. Almost continuous civil war ensues.
2467 A.D.
Islam, 1841 A.D.: The empire's integrity is guaranteed by the Five Powers of Europe. The era of the Ottoman Empire's role as the Sick Man of Europe begins.

2471 A.D.

Islam, 1845 A.D.: Russia begins a campaign for the liberation of the Balkans, thereby starting the Crimean War. Turkey is supported by the French and British.

2477 A.D.

Rome, 350 A.D.: Persians take Armenia.

2481 A.D.

Islam, 1855 A.D.: Russia capitulates, but the Ottoman Empire's hold on the Balkans is loosened.

Commentary

It has been argued that this phase in a civilization's history constitutes a return to the "Heroic Age," the earliest and usually semi-legendary period of a culture's life. In that distant time, the era of Charlemagne and Agamemnon, the world was not a homogenous civilized society. It was a dangerous place, where adventure could easily be found (indeed, it would often come looking for you), but where intrepid men (and the occasional scheming woman) could by their valor place themselves among the demigods. There were, indeed, people living in these later periods who seem to have been foolish enough to believe something similar. Certainly we find rulers such as Julian the Apostate, who tried to turn the Roman Empire back to Diocletian's somewhat fantasticated "old time religion." The Emperor Julian seems to have spent his conscious life planning to imitate Alexander the Great. In the event, of course, his march to the East produced a defeat for Roman arms remarkable even for this epoch of decay. Still, the men loved him, or at least those who wrote memoirs did.

Certainly, it is a good age for panegyrics, and not just at the imperial level. This is one of those times when the irresponsible powerful love to be flattered in historical terms. At any rate, they cultivate what they imagine, sometimes accurately, to be historical styles of art and manners.

Indeed, it sometimes becomes difficult to distinguish the artifacts of this and later periods from those of the earliest times. There was an enormous reproduction of the art of the Old Kingdom in the tombs and ceremonial spaces of the post-imperial period in Egypt, not all of it of negligible quality. The later Empire of the West came to be dominated by a fine if monotonous Gothic. The superiority of twenty-fifth century building materials over their medieval counterparts, however, permitted a revival of stained glass windows that went far beyond anything attempted in the High Middle Ages, either in size or attention to detail. The late empire was, after all, another age of faith.

Some cultures do this kind of thing better than others, of course. One of the sorry features of late Roman civilization, for instance, is the simply incompetent execution of statuary and public building construction. The personal portraiture of the period, especially that executed on colossal scale, usually meant a grotesque caricature of the subject. Triumphal arches (for which there was some call, since most emperors were the victors in civil wars) actually stole bas-reliefs and other fine features from monuments constructed by the rulers of happier times.

Considered as a whole, especially in light of the decrepit state of the imperial economy, there is still a surprising amount of building during this period. Sometimes, of course, this is because the empire partly occupies the territory of a young culture. Spengler, for instance, was of the opinion that Constantine the Great was the first figure in what would later become Islamic culture. He was analogous in some ways to the early Holy Roman Emperors in Western culture, from this point of view. Thus, his vast city building projects, particularly the new capital at Constantinople, drew their energy more from the eastern peoples who were still half primitive than from the nearly exhausted civilization represented by the Roman Empire. Even allowing this to be the case, however, his cities were still cities of the late Classical style; the distinctive Byzantine spirit which would later distinguish them still lay some centuries in the future.

The late Islamic empire itself, the distant heir of Byzantium, lived in a peculiar state of anxiety between its need to arm itself against the West using Western technique and its determination to defend its integrity as a cultural and religious entity against Western intellectual penetration. Because it had already been partly integrated into the world economic system, its economy was in some ways more vital than that of any other of the great empires in the final generations before collapse. The resources available to its government actually increased. Thus, it could pay for, and even initiate the manufacture, of state-of-the-art weapons technology.

None of this was enough, however. The empire could continue to win victories, particularly among insurgent groups in the core areas, but its economy could not grow as fast as that of the weakest Western power. In the final analysis, it could not "modernize," make itself into a creature of the post-Napoleonic West, without ceasing to be what it was. It thus suffered the indignity (shared by several empires in other contexts) of being kept alive until such times as its enemies should be able to decide among themselves how to carve it up. The Turks were remarkable, if anything, for the number of times their performance on the battlefield forced the predatory Great Powers to delay the final act.

Most civilizations during this period do not have even the sometimes dismaying "advantages" offered by an up and coming neighbor anxious to keep them alive for a time. One perfectly real advantage of being in the shadow of a more powerful neighbor, however, is that it greatly concentrates the mind. Thus, some old civilizations such as Egypt and Rome, who had less impressive if still dangerous neighbors, felt free to relax for long periods of time into a number of warring jurisdictions. This was tolerable, perhaps, because the lives of these cultures had in large measure been simplified. Egypt was becoming what it was to be in all future ages, a money machine that shipped staples downstream to the cities of the Delta, which in turn shipped back manufactured items and occasional doses of law and order. Even when no one was actually in charge of the whole system, it had become clear to the whole world that the country was essentially a vast commercial plantation, one that would serve one group of managers as well as another.

In the Roman Empire, the northern strip of territories from the western German border, east and south to Milan (the real capital of the Western Roman Empire), and then around the Adriatic through the Balkans to Constantinople, because a sort of amphitheater of civil war. To the south of this strip there were the major cities, and on the southern rim of the Mediterranean the food producing centers which made life in the rapidly depopulating northern tier possible. From south to north, each tier supported the one above it but was otherwise left to its own devices, so that it was quite possible for reasonable ordinary people to avoid everything to do with the unpleasantness but pay taxes. The unpleasantness could even be justified with the excuse that it kept well-seasoned soldiers within easy striking distance of the dangerous northern frontier (it also tended to make the more chronically dangerous Persian frontier indefensible, but you can't have everything).

The twenty-fifth century Empire of the West, for its part, was less prone to civil war than other civilizations. Like China, it preferred palace coups and long regencies when power was to be transferred in an unorthodox fashion. The two major wars of the period, one launched by an insurgent general, the other by civilian administrators sworn to uphold the interests of an infant emperor whose claim to the throne seemed about to be thrust aside, were fantastic naval conflicts fought by a dozen aircraft carrier groups in the North Atlantic and supported by directed energy weapons from space. The second of these wars resulted in one of the two successful invasions ever to be made of North America. In both these conflicts, civilians even in most of North America were scarcely affected.

Spengler had argued, plausibly at the time, the next great complex of culture and civilization was to arise in Russia. However, there was no Russian Constantine the Great. No nominally Western emperor surreptitiously inaugurated a new Russian world spirit while seeming to preserve the old. The reason was that Napoleon, unlike Alexander, had failed in his drive to the east. Russia's fate was unlike that which the Near East suffered at the hands of Greece. Russia, never conquered from the West, saw its sovereignty simply dissolved into the Western Imperium with that of all other sovereignties at the end of modernity. Unlike Constantine's East, which had been artificially and prematurely urbanized by the spread of Hellenization, Russia became a steadily more provincial region as the Empire of the West matured. Its place in the scheme of things was as a wealthy supplier of grain and raw materials and ambitious emigrants. There was nothing to recommend it as a new base of power for Western rulers, even to those of Russian extraction. Thus no citadel against chaos like Constantinople was established there. There was no counterfeit heart to darken the imagination of a young culture. The final stages of western civilization passed over the steppe like a storm, doing little damage. After it was all over, Russia could begin almost afresh.

Section Four: The End of the World (2481-2520)

"Oh Christian era,
Era of chivalry and the barbarians and the machines,
era of science and the saints,
When you go down make a good sunset.
Never linger superfluous, old and holy and paralytic like India,
Go down in conclusive war and a great sunset,
great age go down..."

--Robinson Jeffers
  I Shall Laugh Purely

Readout

2484 A.D.
China, 184 A.D.: Taoist millenarians, the Yellow Turbans, devastate the empire.
2487 A.D.
Rome, 360 A.D.: Huns invade Europe.
2501 A.D.
Islam, 1875 A.D.: Risings against the Turks in the Balkans.
2502 A.D.
Islam, 1876 A.D.: Abdul Hamid comes to power, the last Sultan to rule effectively.
2503 A.D.
Islam, 1877 A.D.: Russia invades the Balkans.
2504 A.D.
Islam, 1878 A.D. The Congress of Berlin preserves the Ottoman Empire, at the cost of lessened sovereignty.
2505 A.D.
Rome, 375 A.D.: Visigoths defeat and kill the Emperor Valens at the Battle of Adrianople. The empire never regains control of its borders.

2519 A.D.
Rome, 392 A.D.: The Emperor Theodosius the Great comes to power, the last emperor to rule both halves of the empire.
2520 A.D.
China, 220 A.D.: The last Han emperor abdicates.

Commentary

The only great empire which came to an official end during this period was that of the Latter Han, yet all (save Egypt) receive their death blow at this time. In principle, the chief precipitating causes are barbarian invasions and internal revolt. So familiar to civilization have the barbarian peoples become by this time, however, and so alienated from the imperial authority have the populations of certain anciently civilized districts grown, that the distinction between them is often of small practical significance. This is not true of most of the empire's subjects, of course, but the level of alienation is enough to bring down the system. The empire dies because a decisive minority of the peoples of the world it governs no longer identify with it. They see its resources simply as booty.

The majority, impoverished and dwindling in number as population contracts, have long since come to see statecraft and the defense of the empire as the special concern of a class of predatory rulers. They feel no more inclined to work or fight for the maintenance of the imperial regime than country people would be to volunteer to help an exclusive riding club hunt for foxes.

There is, of course, a great deal of hypocrisy and simple confusion in the attitude of both the empire's friends and enemies. The end of the empire as a political event is unimaginable to almost everyone, from the barbarian invaders to the emperor's speechwriters. So long has it existed that its end seems indistinguishable from the end of the world. Occasionally, as in China and the West, the forces which effectively kill the empire in this period are trying to achieve exactly that. More often, however, the barbarians are seeking an autonomy within the empire, recognized by the universal government, and sweetened by "subsidies" which soon become simple payments of tribute. Even the Greeks who repeatedly attempted to bring down the Ottoman Empire envisioned what in essence would have been a revival of the Byzantine Empire, ruled from Istanbul and including not only Greece but both shores of the Aegean and wide regions of Anatolia.

Those who support the empire, who constitute the majority of its people even in the worst cases, similarly equate the collapse of the central authority with intolerable chaos. This loyalty is usually a matter of abstract principle, however. They cheat on their taxes and avoid conscription in droves when the government is foolish enough to attempt it. These things are increasingly easy to do as the bureaucracy suffers more and more from interruptions in communication and the corruption that comes from fixed prices and wages in an inflationary environment. They may, and usually do, hate and fear the current emperor, the provincial governor, or some oppressive policy which applies to their religious or ethnic group. Still, in their mental universe the empire is the guardian of everything good in human life, of learning and the cherished art of the past, of religion and law and justice. The system is too diffuse, however, and the implications of its downfall too incomprehensible, for this sentiment to solidify into anything like the aggressive nationalism of modernity. Individuals and whole cities will perform prodigies of courage and ingenuity to defend their regions and their interests. The empire as a whole, except for a tiny minority with some professional reason to think about its fate systematically, is literally too important to defend.

The fatal misfortunes to which the universal states are subject are various, but such is the similarity of their fates that these events are clearly only occasions for some deeper, common process to manifest itself. It was in the Roman Empire, perhaps, where the blow seemed to be most purely military. For some time, barbarian peoples had been drifting south across the northern border. Often they would be brusquely turned back or, more and more, settled on wasteland inside the border on Roman terms. Eventfully, in the last quarter of the fourth century, an authorized influx of Gothic peoples from north of the Danube went on a rampage because of Roman maladministration and corruption. The army sent to put down this rebellion (since the people were for the most part already on Roman soil, it was hardly an invasion) was led by the emperor himself. To everyone's surprise, not least the barbarians', the Roman army was defeated before the city of Adrianople and the Goths left free, at least briefly, to pillage in the Balkans.

While a degree of control was again established in the northern tier of the empire, the imperial forces were sometimes mere traffic police for new immigrants. The newcomers were only nominally subjects of the empire; the central government treated with their leaders to ensure they would do as little damage as possible to the precariously-supplied cities. By swift degrees, the imperial government passed from the status of ruler to hegemon to referee of the peoples and cities north of the Mediterranean.

The Ottomans, not altogether dissimilarly, reached the stage during this period when they were no longer masters of their own house. Despite their long occupation of the Balkans, few universal states seem to have been so widely and persistently disliked by its subject peoples as the Turks were by a majority of the people in that area. It was, perhaps, precisely because the empire's policy had always been to respect the ethnic and religious identities of its subjects, to keep their essences distinct, that the sort of nationalist animosities which had long since disappeared in other late civilizations were still so virulent in this one. Left to itself, the Balkan revolt of the period, decisively aided by the Russians, could have brought the Ottoman story to an abrupt end. As it was, the execution of the empire was suspended by the Congress of Berlin. Its provinces were disposed of by foreigners of alien culture, while its core territory was increasingly the site of Western enterprises and projects. The Sultan's authority was secure only over those core areas of Anatolia where his own ethnic group predominated. Even the Muslim Arabs to the south were becoming restless. If the Roman Empire could struggle on for a century longer because of the ignorance and incompetence of its barbarians, the Ottoman Empire survived only a bit more than a generation on the sufferance of the West.

In China, we have an appallingly clear example of a civilization which tried, with some success, to bring its own life to an end by blowing itself up. History runs in great cycles, according to Chinese and some Western philosophers. Toward the end of a cycle, the world grows so old and corrupt that the only thing to do with it is to destroy it. According to the Yellow Turban Society of the Latter Han Dynasty, the duty to do this lay with a vanguard. Only a minority of them would survive the destruction, but those who did would become the Seed People of the new age. If the Yellow Turbans were revolutionaries, then they were insurgents after the manner of Pol Pot rather than Lenin, or even than the eschatologically-minded T'ai P'ing rebellion of the nineteenth century. Destruction was the goal and genocide was the instrument.

The Yellow Turban rebellion itself was actually put down in fairly short order. In western China, on the other hand, the Five Pecks of Rice Taoists, who harbored similar sentiments, maintained a sort of millenarian kingdom for thirty years. In any event, the rebellion inaugurated a period of general disorder and indiscipline which the imperial government was wholly incompetent to stem. The last of the Han emperors abdicated at the "suggestion" of his chief general. A curious twilight period followed, during which the depopulated and ravaged civilized world did not yet collapse, but had no visible means of support.

In the West, where time was more often seen as linear than cyclical, the Joachite Rebellion of the early twenty-sixth century actually intended to end human history once and for all. The ideology of this catastrophic cult (which eventually claimed more than half-a-billion adherents) incorporated Marxist elements in a framework provided by the eschatological ideas of the twelfth century abbot, Joachim of Fiore. The time since Christ, according to the movement's prophets, had actually been the Millennium of the Book of Revelation. The Evil One had been imprisoned, his power for harm limited, for 2520 years (seven "perfect" years of 360 days, each day represented by a year in turn; a cosmic week). This epoch saw the victory of Socialism, the most just form of society imaginable in this world. In essence, the age of universal government (even with its free market features) had been the embodiment of the Kingdom of God. Had it not been created precisely by the victory of the people over world finance and national obscurantism? Sometimes the Kingdom had been purer, sometimes more tainted, but it had certainly reached its peak during the era of the universal state. Since that polity was obviously coming to an end, it was clear that the Evil One had been released from his prison for a short while. The synthesis of culture and politics and science which had been achieved after modernity was now

142

exhausted. The time had come to make the world into the beautiful desert described in the last chapters of Revelation. The Elect and the Elect alone would survive to build the New Jerusalem. There would be no other men and no other habitation in all the world.

The New Jerusalem came into being as an insurgents camp in the Midwest of what had been the United States. For the decades in which the insurgency survived, however, it became the capital of a ghostly polity with outposts on every continent. Half of the urbanized areas of the world were destroyed either by the insurgents themselves (who included a quarter of the mutinous armed forces), or by the desperate and confused imperial government. Among the other dreadful features of the period was the only extensive use of nuclear weapons since the First Transition which ended modernity. The imperial regime finally succeeded in restoring "order" over a civilized world which in large part had ceased to exist.

Afterlife: (2520-2603)

"Do not expect too much of the end of the world."

---*Stanislaw J. Lec*

Readout

2521 A.D.
China, 221 A.D.: The empire is divided into three, with spasmodic attempts at reunion.
2523 A.D.
Islam, 1897 A.D.: The Greeks try to take Crete from the Turks.
2525 A.D.
Rome, 398 A.D.: Alaric the Visigoth plunders Athens.
2534 A.D.
Islam, 1908 A.D.: The Young Turks take control of the empire in a coup.
2535 A.D.
Islam, 1909 A.D.: The Young Turks install Mohammed V as Sultan.
2537 A.D.
Rome, 410 A.D.: Alaric sacks Rome.
Islam, 1911 A.D.: The Italians defeat the Turks and take Tripoli and Cyrenacia.
2538 A.D.
Islam, 1912 A.D.: The empire loses further ground in a general Balkan war.
2539 A.D.
Islam, 1913 A.D.: The empire somewhat recoups its position in a second Balkan War.
2540 A.D.
Islam, 1914 A.D.: The First World War begins, and the empire fights with the Central Powers of Europe.

2544 A.D.

Islam, 1918 A.D.: The Central Powers lose the war. The empire suffers dismemberment by the victorious European alliance.

2546 A.D.

Rome, 419 A.D.: Minority of Valentinian III under the regency of his mother, Galla Placidia.

2548 A.D.

Islam, 1922 A.D.: Mustafa Kemal declares a republic in Anatolia, ending the empire.

2552 A.D.

Rome, 425 A.D.: Barbarians overrun the West, mostly to settle.

2556 A.D.

Rome, 429 A.D.: Gaiseric founds a Vandal Kingdom in North Africa.

2560 A.D.

Rome, 433 A.D.: Attila becomes king of the Huns.

2563 A.D.

Rome, 436 A.D.: Last Roman troops leave Britain.

2565 A.D.

China, 265 A.D.: Northern China is overrun by barbarians.

2582 A.D.

Rome, 455 A.D.: Vandals sack Rome.

2587 A.D.

Rome 460 A.D.: Cologne captured by the Franks.

2602 A.D.

Egypt, 945 B.C.: Sheshonk I of Libya establishes the Twenty-Second Dynasty. A raid is made into Palestine.

2603 A.D.

Rome, 476 A.D.: The child emperor Romulus Augustulus abdicates, ending the empire in the West.

Commentary

The latter days of the Austro-Hungarian Empire, it is said, were very merry. "The situation is hopeless but not serious" was the catchword as the Austrians munched their amazing pastries and plotted to occupy Serbia. The end of the universal states has always been accompanied by a mood different from this. It is everywhere a time of mourning and distress, of people who know that their societies are less than those of their grandfathers, and who know that their grandchildren will live in a world more degraded still. Much later historians are often inclined to point out the continuities between the period before the collapse and the period after. Universal states, indeed, governments of any description which control a wide area, are less common in history than we might think. The collapse can be looked on as a return to normality.

Maybe, but such a view is antihistorical, imposing the perceptions of later times onto the people of the past. For themselves, the Chinese and the Romans and the Turks knew that the world was going to Hell in a handbasket, dammit. What they valued in their world was not always what we value in it, but still they saw there was less and less to be proud of in their age. The date that is picked for "the end of the empire" is always somewhat arbitrary. It is generally a political marker for a transformation in demographics, the economy and the spiritual state of mankind which takes several decades to occur. Indeed, as skeleton civilizations, what Spengler called "fellah societies" (after the fellahin peasants of Egypt), universal states may go on indefinitely.

The Egyptian civilization never ended. At least another eight dynasties can be named from the histories of the region, until it became a province of the Roman Empire. Even then, Egypt never completely ceased to be Egypt, though language and even the ethnic makeup of the country changed more than once. However, after the phase under examination here, the dynasties are more and more of foreign origin. Even when natives ruled, they were interested in business rather than sovereignty, since

146

Egypt soon became the great factory and breadbasket of the Mediterranean world. With few exceptions, these pharaohs were vassals of powerful empires to the east, and the indigenous culture the pharaohs promoted was a mummified replica of the art and architecture of the Old Kingdom. From this point, there was no special story in what was going on. To the extent that Egyptian history was meaningful thereafter, the meaning was provided by its relationship to still vital societies.

The Ottoman Empire was perhaps unique in precipitating its own end and primarily through the folly of its rulers. The Westernizing Young Turk clique was trying to do the impossible, to make a modern European nation of an ancient universal state. Themselves half-westerners, cultural hybrids of the sort who would do so much harm to the so-called "Third World" during the twentieth and twentieth-first centuries, they despised their own culture without having a particularly profound grasp of their acquired one. When put to the test in the First World War, the haphazardly-modernized empire flew into roughly the components from which it had been assembled five hundred years before. Unlike the case in other post-imperial periods, there was no particular nostalgia among the empire's former subjects for its return. Even to people living in the Magian heartlands, to Greeks and Jews and Armenians, the empire was always a Turkish affair, the possession of another people. This was the nature of Islamic statecraft, to maintain distinctions among nationalities. On the other hand, precisely because the Turks had kept themselves distinct, they were also unique among post-imperial peoples in achieving a new type of political cohesion on a more modest scale. The Republic of Turkey, however, is really a creature of Western civilization rather than Islam.

The end of Han China was sad and confused. The empire as a whole, with its Great Wall and strategic passes, was perhaps defensible against the barbarians from Central Asia; certainly that had been one of the chief preoccupations of the imperial government since before the Latter Han period began. The feuding successor states, with their pretensions to be the true heirs of the Han, were not defensible. The ancient centers of Chinese civilization in the north were depopulated by war, famine and disease. The south was wealthier and often able to maintain an effective defense, but there was no possibility of reconstituting a universal order. Civilization and barbarism mixed, as they have in many places and many times. This cycle of human experience came to a fairly decisive end.

The end of the Roman Empire offered a Vandal's delight of portable booty and former imperial citizens perfectly willing to be enserfed. In these last decades, one may speak of true "invasions" and "campaigns" by the barbarians. They were no longer infiltrations and piratical raids by primitives. The later barbarian hordes were at least as competent as the Roman armies sent to oppose them, and in fact made up of much the same ethnic mix of people, since the empire had long since taken to doing most of its recruiting among accommodating newcomers. More to the point, the barbarians had a clear strategic plan: they had come first to rob and them to settle, and they had a fair notion of where they wanted to do both.

As was the case in China, half of the empire, the east in this case, was able to put up substantial resistance, at any rate enough to prevent the establishment of barbarian kingdoms in the hinterlands of Constantinople. Indeed, as we have noted, this eastern (or Byzantine) empire was to become the beginning of a story that ended only with the collapse of the Ottoman Empire 1500 years later. The story at hand, however, the one told by the civilization which began with the Trojan War and extended to the fifth century A.D., ends on an inglorious note. In the final phase of the Western Roman Empire, the emperor never stirs beyond the heavily defended city of Milan if he can help it, while one after another of the great cities of the West fall to societies of organized bandits. In the end, the Church comes to provide what there is of civil administration as the imperial government loses even nominal control of the provinces. Because the imperial office has long been a mere front for generals of barbarian origin, the end can be undramatic; there is no need to make a fuss over the forms when the substance has long leached away. The guardians of a child emperor simply decide that it would be safer just to abdicate than to go through the motions of another long regency.

The end of the Empire of the West in the early twenty-seventh century was attended by a slogan: "Cutting the losses." Everywhere, there were great stretches of continent that had passed out of civilized life altogether. The regime's guiding policy was to prevent the extinction of the species, and to ensure the survival of the classic books and the canon of science. Wherever possible, it encouraged the concentration of population by those living in lightly-peopled countries, a description which fit most of the planet. There was no coercion in any of this; the imperial government had neither the power nor the heart to ever coerce anyone ever again. Their theory, probably correct, was simply that civilized life required a certain density of people.

The regime in its final stages maintained a dozen or so "cities," really fortified schools and trading posts, constructed in the delicate Twilight Romanesque of the lattermost West. Except to the extent that it pursued the bands of terrible New People, created at the whim of the mad Emperor Friedrich in the twenty-fourth century, the government did not even attempt police functions beyond its own facilities.

Indeed, it appeared that, having lost the whole world, Earth's ostensible rulers were intent upon saving their own souls. The imperial government itself had lost its military character, since every conceivable organized enemy had ceased to exist. The leadership of mankind had become a purely ceremonial post. The Western emperors had in fact been powerless for almost a century. Latterly, the office had tended to devolve on some scholar or member of the imperial civil service, coincident with his retirement. The administrative apparatus developed a character like that of a religious order or a university faculty. Indeed, it eventfully did become largely clericalized: the fossil West had returned to the ancient image of politics as a dialogue between pope and emperor.

Partly because of the Joachite Wars, and partly because of the natural decrease in population, there were fewer than a quarter of a billion people on Earth by the year 2600. There were perhaps three hundred thousand in all the surviving planetary colonies put together. In this epoch, the population of Luna City, always essentially an appendage of terrestrial society, was evacuated to Earth. A scattering of human settlements around the ice mines of the lunar north elected to remain, despite the fact Earth's rapid loss of space technology would surely make the decision permanent. The almost purely scientific outposts on Mercury, and the troubled colonies in the treacherous environment of Mars, never had the option of returning.

The Last Emperor of the West, in active life a teacher of comparative mathematics and systematic theology at the University of Chicago, died in his sleep in the year 2601 A.D. The College of Electors gathered from the four corners of the world for the last time to consider the choice of a successor. They adjourned without taking action, sine die.

The last line rolls up and off the screen, which for a moment remains blank. Then, quite without prompting, another line of text appears:

Welcome to Dr. Spengler's Temporal Analogizer.

About the author and publisher

John J. Reilly (1954 - 2012). Son of Jean Reilly and John Reilly. After graduating from St. Peter's College and earning his law degree from Georgetown University, he embarked upon a career as a writer, editor and attorney. Sometimes that was as a legal editor, sometimes as a polemicist, and sometimes as an unaffiliated but not wholly unrespectable scholar.

His keen intellect and wry sense of humor resulted in many publications and a world-wide network of correspondents. His intellectual preoccupations ranged from theology and in particular eschatology to politics, alternative history, and the philosophy of science and literature. During his life he published four books including *Spengler's Future*, *The Perennial Apocalypse*, *Apocalypse and Future*, and *The Perfection of the West*. John regularly appeared in First Things, Kirkus Review, and had been an editor at Culture Wars before he withdrew in protest to a drift toward anti-Semitism which he publicly denounced.

John also maintained a blog, The Long View, where he serenely surveyed the world and opined that, indeed, everything is going to be OK. John's intellectual interests also expressed themselves in various societies in which he was active including The International Society for the Comparative Study of Civilizations, the Center for Millennial Studies, the Simplified Spelling Society, and American Literacy Counsel.

A man of breathtakingly ecumenical feeling, he was without compromise a true and devout Catholic. John explained himself thusly: "After long thought, I realized that the most important thing in life is to be helpful. So, I have taken to explaining things, carefully and empathetically, and often at very great length 'Spengler with a Smile' is how I usually characterize the organizing principle."

Benjamin I. Espen preserved John's website and books after his death, and republishes John's writings with the permission of John's estate. Ben also publishes book reviews and literary criticism at his blog hosted at http://www.benespen.com/

Made in the USA
Columbia, SC
21 May 2023

16444891R10088